You Don't Change A Company By Memo

You Don't Change A Company By Memo

The Simple Truths About Managing Change

Marti Smye, Ph.D.
with
Anne McKague

KEY PORTER·BOOKS

This book is dedicated to two guys I love,
Josh and Matt, with the hope that by the time
you enter the workforce books like this won't be
necessary. This book is also dedicated to my
friend and mentor, Mr. Ed Lang for his
continuous advice and counsel.

Copyright © 1994 Dr. Marti Smye and Anne McKague

All rights reserved. No part of this work covered by the copyrights hereon may be reproduced or used in any form or by any means — graphic, electronic or mechanical, including photocopying, recording, taping or information storage and retrieval systems — without the prior written permission of the publisher, or, in case of photocopying or other reprographic copying, without a licence from the Canadian Reprography Collective.

Canadian Cataloguing in Publication Data

Smye, Marti D., 1950–
    You don't change a company by memo : the simple
    truths about managing change
ISBN 1-55013-616-X

1. Organizational change.   I. McKague, Anne.
II. Title.

HD58.8.858   1994   658.4'06   C94-932083-8

The publisher gratefully acknowledges the assistance of the Canada Council and the Government of Ontario.

Key Porter Books Limited
70 The Esplanade
Toronto, Ontario
Canada M5E 1R2

Distributed in the United States of America by National Book Network, Inc. 1-800-462-6420

Printed and bound in Canada

95 96 97 98 99 5 4 3 2

Acknowledgements

This book was written with the people who are out there in the world making change happen. At People Tech I work with teams who actually go into companies every day. As chair of the board, I'm denied direct access to the excitement, although I often have the honor of supporting a particular chairman.

So most of this book belongs to others at People Tech who are experiencing the considerable satisfactions of helping leaders on a day-to-day basis. One of the main contributors is Jim McCloskey, who quietly works his way around the world making change happen.

There are many others:

The people who came to the cottage: Norm Johnston, Rick Lash, Treat Hull and the president of People Tech, Don Hathaway. The people who made us comfortable at the cottage: Barb Abbott and Jean Hachie.

People who gave inspired time: Jane Lindsay-Laberge, Anne Stephens, Margaret Smith, Richard Zuliani, Ellen Cohen, Gundy Chambers, Bill McKendree, Tom Bell, Lorne Hartman, Susan Dunn, Connie Phenix, Anita Shilton, Rick Anderson, Murray Wade and Bonnie Webster.

Anne McKague, whose name appears on the cover, and the other people who made the thoughts, opinions, ideas and real work in the real world into a book: Philippa

Campsie, Patrick Withrow, Becky Vogan, Michaela Koch, Sylvie Tremblay, Sarah Withrow, Rae Ann Bryson and Howard Shulman.

People who read: Anne Golden, Glenna Carr, Judith John and Lori Northrup; and people who researched: Wendy Potter, Lora Garrett, Kathy Jennings and Stephanie Saville.

The magic in my life delivered two other people without whom I never could have completed this book. One is the project coordinator: my publicist, Lise Hutchinson. She is willing to talk to the President of the United States or the manager of any maintenance unit. She brought together resources from heaven and, despite provocation, did not kill me with "a little sword made of rusted sardine tin lids." The other is Zella Hayman, a blessed person who runs my work and my life and lets me appear as a rational and complete person.

There are also the people who granted us the time to interview them; their experience demonstrates the reality of the theories here.

The list ends with the agents at Sterling Lord: Linda McKnight and Bruce Westwood, who believed in this project from the start.

Later in this book, you'll read how many people you need to help you make effective change. I'm amazed by the number it took to simply write about it in an organized and effective manner.

Contents

Introducing Dr. Change

Allow me to get the credentials out of the way: Dr. Marti Smye holds a doctorate in Applied Psychology, she has a Master's of Education in Adult Education and Counseling, she writes a management column for the *Globe and Mail*'s Report on Business, and she's a popular and entertaining public speaker in Canada and the United States. Dr. Smye chairs the board at People Tech, a management consulting company that specializes in planning, implementing and accelerating large-scale organizational change and transformation. The company is active during restructuring, mergers, acquisitions, rapid growth or downsizing, business turnarounds and privatization. Dr. Smye's company has a long list of blue-chip clients, including Hostess Frito-Lay, Pepsi-Cola, Campbell Soup Company, Aetna Life and Casualty, Royal Insurance, Continental Insurance, IBM, Kraft-Jacobs Suchard, Union Bank of Switzerland and CIBA Vision.

That sounds like a lot, and it is — but it is important to understand that while her academic background is impeccable, it is her experience helping dozens of corporations to cope with massive changes that is the real source of her insights and advice. Take these observations, for example:

- Falling trade barriers and the resulting access to new markets demand a global outlook. Corporations face competition from an expanding number of players.

- Traditional organization structures often have built-in problems that make them inflexible and slow to respond — deadly sins in the fast-paced global economy.

- Competitive organizations are necessarily flatter, flexible, responsive and dynamic. They put decisions in the hands of the employees dealing with their customers, and they learn from their mistakes. They are obsessed with service and improvement.

- Any practical approach to change acknowledges the realities of the workplace and the abilities and attitudes of the people who work there. Understand that it is the individuals in your workforce who will be driving the change, and that leadership is about navigation. It is not about who is at the wheel, who gets a window seat or who owns the car.

Marti believes that getting there should be more than half the fun. She knows that one of the workplace realities is that it occupies a major part of the lives of the people who work there. She believes that if people are given a supportive, caring and engaging environment to work in, they will give their whole minds to their jobs and gain satisfaction from doing so. The concept is simple — but fulfilling it often requires massive and profound adjustments of a fundamental and corporation-wide nature.

High levels of corporate angst have spawned a "change management" industry, and perhaps this is what's needed if leaders are to find the help and ideas they need. But the business world is suddenly faced with a lot of newly minted experts, and "caveat emptor" is sound advice. Marti, on the other hand, created "Dr. Change" as a device to speak from experience — her best credential. She prefers to show rather than tell, and the ideas flow from her career of helping companies cut the Gordian knot of change. So do seek this doctor's advice, but don't expect it to be dressed up in jargon, or particularly kind — that is not Marti's style, and it would not help you in any case.

Don't expect paradigms to shift between the pages of this book. Do expect to learn about change and how to deal with it, in terms of what to do on Monday morning. It is much easier that way. More efficient. More Marti.

Because you are busy, I know you will thank her for being prescriptive, bold and blunt. In your search for the best solutions and initiatives, take the advice of the good doctor.

The first thing she will help you change is your mind,

a thousand times in all the little ways you see your work-force and the dynamics of your company — both internal and external — in this ever-changing world.

And that is why you should read this book. That is why Marti wrote it.

Don Hathaway
President, People Tech

P.S.: My credentials? I work for the lady; I speak from first-hand experience.

An Owner's Manual for This Book

The reason you're reading this book is to write your own. Your book will be called something like *"How I Brought* (put the name of your company here) *into the 21st Century, Thrashing, Squealing and Profiting.*

You *have* to write your own book on change management: no two organizations are alike, no two are at the same stage of maturity, no two are facing the same issues. Your book has to be different.

What we've written will help, and more than just a little. This book has been written by people who have survived the exhilarating/frustrating/maddening/satisfying process of change in dozens of organizations. They've made the mistakes — and know how to avoid them. They've attained the successes — and know how to work to ensure them. Their experience will save you years, and perhaps an unattractive dependence on Gelusil. All those failures and all those successes, all the hints that make change work better, all the checklists that real change in a real corporation demands — they're all here.

Getting Started

Here's how I'd suggest you use this book:

- Get yourself a fat three-ring binder full of blank pages. On the cover write, "Making the change at (name of your company)." Alternately, dedicate a special section of your laptop's memory to the project: a *big* section.

- Divide the binder or the byte bin into the same sections we've divided this book into.

- Read the book once, fast. That'll give you a good feel for where we may be going together.

- Then read it slowly, over a period of a month or so. Most of the book consists of pieces you can read in under five minutes. Read each brief idea, think about how it applies to your organization and then start writing down rough notes.

- Keep asking yourself questions: "*How* will I do this? *When*? *Who* will help?" And keep your notes: when you've finished the book, those notes will be the basis for your change plan. If you do the job right, you should end up with the most comprehensive, coherent and bullet-proof change plan of anyone in your organization.

* Send us a copy.

Giraffes and Strategy

Before we get started, I'd like to say a word or two about jargon. Management books are usually dripping with the stuff, and sometimes it's hard to keep all those similar-sounding words straight. In a company I visited recently, I found a poster that gave serious-sounding definitions to terms such as values, purpose, vision, mission, key objectives, strategy and operating principles, presumably because no one there could keep them straight either. (Considering that this document defined a mission as a "meta-objective," I'm not sure how useful it was anyway.)

As with all overworked terms, most of the meaning has long since leached out of these words. People who write books on management have to come up with new combinations (Mastering the Key Objectives of Strategic Missions, or Visioning the Purpose of Values), or invent a whole new vocabulary (animal metaphors are particularly popular — Jitterbugging with the Giraffes, or Teaching the Dolphins to Suck Eggs). It's well meant and all, but confusing. One day you're going to find yourself trying to jitterbug with a strategic value, and then where will you be?

In this book, I have tried to use plain language as much as possible. Not only does the jargon bore me to death, but using it obscures the fact that change is a lot easier to talk about than it is to do, and there's no point making it sound even harder than it has to. After all, at some point you have to put this and all your other books down and get on with it. You won't be able to hide behind feel-good slogans or cute animal analogies, so why should I?

"Who's talking here?"

Checking my appointment books for the past few years, I note that I've been heavily involved in the realities of changing corporations. There's a string of meetings with a multinational in Switzerland that had to transform itself in order to get ready to market in the former Soviet Union. There's a long period of concentrated effort in Hartford, Connecticut, that was spent planning and implementing the changes an insurance company wanted to make to get ready for a new kind of consumer. There are speeches about change management to groups in Hong Kong, Toronto, Dallas, Lake Tahoe and New York. There are client conferences with AT&T, Campbell Soup, IBM, army officers of the Czech republic, governments — all about changing their organizations to match the changes in competition, markets and economic reality.

There are two dozen people at People Tech. They all have appointment books similar to mine. And that's made People Tech an intriguing and energizing place to work in the past 15 years. We get together and examine how change is effected in different organizations in different ways. There are some strange synergies: what worked for a snack-food company ends up helping a quasi-governmental organization 14 hours of flying time away. The same bureaucratic diseases that weaken a century-old market leader have begun infecting a software firm formed just a decade ago.

It's interesting to walk down the halls of one of our three offices. There's a definite excitement, a feeling of being on the leading edge, a profound sense that what's wrong with the traditional organization can be put right and that companies, employees and consumers will all gain from the metamorphosis. There's also the more-than-occasional look of frustration: change can be painful, and it never happens at the speed its instigators want.

I can't imagine a more satisfying place to work — or more interesting people to work with. As you read, remember that this book is all of them talking through me: the people at People Tech and all our clients around the world. What they say is interesting — and they speak with authority.

You Don't Change A Company By Memo

CHAPTER ONE

No Pain, No Change

Today's organization and what's going on to survive
tomorrow

·

Three kinds of pain

·

Getting your people to recognize (huh?) pain

"The ability to learn faster than your competitors may be
the only sustainable competitive advantage."

ARIE DE GEUS, FORMER GROUP PLANNING COORDINATOR, ROYAL DUTCH SHELL

IT WAS AN INVITATION I couldn't refuse. I once went
on a dusty visit to an abandoned buggywhip factory on
the border between Vermont and Quebec. The place was
vast: three or four huge stories lit by grimy windows. Up
on the third story I found what I guess must have been the
bookkeepers' desk. The thing must have been 15 feet
long, and from the height of it, it was obvious that the
people who worked at that desk would have had to sit on
stools. I could imagine eyeshades and the scratch of steel

pens. There were a few remaining bills scattered on the desk; whether they were ever sent I don't know.

And there was a worn rubber stamp. Because of the dimness and because the lettering on the stamp was reversed, I had to take it out into the sunlight before I could read it:

"Prosperity will return with the horse."

They probably stamped that motto on all their letters. And they probably had that stamp made at the urging of some president who, no doubt, has been resting under the Vermont clay a long time. It would have been about 1930, when the Depression was really beginning to gnaw.

That stamp represents the ultimate resistance to change: a confident assertion that the rest of the world is wrong, and a quiet hope that world will soon get a grip on itself so that people can get back to what they were doing, the same way they've been doing it.

I've seen organizations take similar attitudes and actions. You've seen it too. Some of them have gone the way of the buggywhip. This book is about the other ones — those that realized times had changed for good, and changed themselves to survive. What caused these companies to contemplate the kind of changes they made? The answers are as different as the organizations.

Sometimes the external world provides catalysts for

change, such as mergers or dramatic business reversals (for example, a new government regulation makes a product obsolete). We can be led to change by forecasts of an inevitable future change ("cars are replacing buggies") that must be responded to, whether the business likes it or not. Change may be necessary because it is getting harder and harder to deliver the results that are expected each year by doing the same things (running faster and faster to stay in the same place).

A model that appeared in *Business Week* (I love it when the media do my work for me) nicely describes the changes that People Tech has observed in workplaces that are realizing success.

	From:	**To:**
Organization	Hierarchy	Network
Structure	Self-sufficiency	Interdependencies
Worker expectations	Security	Personal growth
Leadership	Autocratic	Inspirational
Quality	What's affordable	No compromises
Workforce	Homogeneous	Culturally diverse
Work	By individuals	By teams
Governance	Board of directors	Varied constituencies
Focus	Profits	Customers
Markets	Domestic	Global
Advantage	Cost	Time
Resources	Capital	Information

Look over the list and think about your own organization. None of these changes is easy. All of them mean that somebody's ox gets gored.

"When your company is in trouble, you might not be doing anything wrong in a traditional sense. The world has changed, and you must change with it."

PURDY CRAWFORD, CHAIRMAN AND CEO, IMASCO

Linking Pain to the Need to Change

No matter what brings us to change, the common and overriding experience of change is pain. Change is painful for all people, and in order to convince our people to commit to change, we have to make a powerful case that *the pain of changing will be less than the pain of staying the same.*

Think of things you've changed about yourself. You changed your haircut when you overheard someone making fun of the old one. You changed the way you organized your work because you found that someone else was out-organizing you. You changed the way you eat or drink because it was slowing you down or embarrassing you.

You felt some pain. You made a change because the pain of changing was less than the pain of staying the same.

What's enough pain? Kraft General Foods' snack-food business was watching its margins decrease. Competition from a Frito-Lay company was the cause — even though Kraft General Foods was still the lowest-cost manufacturer and still number one in share. Those decreasing margins hurt enough that leader Ron Tomlinson knew his company had to change. What solution did his team came up with? A merger. It was a painful solution but it was less painful than remaining the same.

What *isn't* enough pain? About eight years ago one of the leaders of a division of Metropolitan Life — "Mother Met" — looked down the road and saw sales going down and profitability disappearing. However the current data were great: the company was making a lot of money. There was no pain — and no impetus to change. The organization's leader had to actually cause pain. He crafted a real and frightening scenario of what the organization would look like five, ten and twenty years in the future. It was only after he carefully put together that scenario that the pain became great enough to allow the needed changes.

For you to detect pain in your current strategic plan you have to be sensitive to thorns like declining profit, customer defections, higher costs of doing business or a high turnover. And then you have to ask yourself: does it hurt enough yet? To assess the answer; look at yourself, at your team and the rest of the people in the organization. You and your team will probably recognize pain before your people do, because pain doesn't usually come suddenly. Your people may have gotten used to it as it increases bit by bit. Or, like an alcoholic, they may have built up an ever-growing set of excuses to mask the pain. It's your job to ask the hard questions and demonstrate the dangers.

Just as pain is incremental, so the response to pain should be incremental. The pain of a business crunch calls for change, but how you deal with the pain should be based on the cause of that pain. Only a careful diagnosing of your working environment can produce an appropriate response and prompt an appropriate process for implementing your changes.

The theory of inertia explains the resistance to change: bodies at rest tend to stay at rest, bodies in motion tend to stay in motion. Getting your corporate body in motion is what change is all about, but you may need to use persuasion to make the case for change, the way Metropolitan Life did. It took the excruciating pain of a long and deep recession to convince many companies that change was needed.

If you and your team aren't the first to spot the pain, somebody else will be. Heroes typically step forward — amongst staff, customers or shareholders. You've read the results in several headline cases lately. The leader was pushed — or ousted altogether.

> **"We must respond to rapid change, or die; it's the law of nature."**
>
> PETER MAURICE, VICE-CHAIR,
>
> CANADA TRUST FINANCIAL SERVICES

How Does It Hurt?

At People Tech, we've found there are three main types of pain that form the essential reasons for change.

The first type is *current pain*: major problems that are right in your face. You're a container company that's suddenly losing a million a week. You're an accounting firm that's suddenly been toppled from its place in the hierarchy because two smaller firms have merged and taken your spot. Your biggest account has just issued a press release that starts, "After many fruitful years of association . . ." Current pain means you should have started yesterday.

The second type is *foreseen pain:* problems that are predicted, but can still be avoided if there's a quick response. Some newspapers saw that the business of setting type in metal wasn't going to be practical in the electronic future. Instead of bits of metal there'd be bytes of information. But they knew that the leap in technology wouldn't be painless. It would require sizeable investments in technology and the downsizing of unionized work forces. Foreseen pain means that you've got to start today or face the consequences. I.e., in a plant where people aren't happy — complaints, discontent — you can take action.

The third type is *inertia pain*. Everything seems fine today, but when you look at coming changes in the world, the market or the customer base, you are concerned that your current business practices aren't going to make it: change is needed now to prepare for tomorrow. Inertia pain means you have to plan for tomorrow — before it gets here.

And Does It Hurt Enough Yet?

"CEO's must recognize that they must do something as difficult as they are asking their people to do. They must understand the pain. Just saying 'I'm going to command change and here is my new vision' is easy. What's hard is to challenge yourself, to put aside assumptions, to take a fresh approach and figure out how you yourself will add value to the organization."

ZOË BAIRD, SENIOR VICE-PRESIDENT AND GENERAL COUNSEL

LAW AND REGULATORY AFFAIRS

AETNA LIFE & CASUALTY COMPANY

Change management is about pain management: to help deal with the roots of the pain, you've got to call on all your resources — the leaders, the management team, the grassroots of your organization — as well as external resources. You have to establish a consensus on the need for change. Here are a number of ways to do it:

The leader and management team feel pain and understand the case for change, but the rest of the organization doesn't.

- Communicate the case — don't hesitate to repeat yourself.

  At People Tech, we've learned how to communicate the case in several ways — and you may have to use several. A favorite is to hold an intense retreat. In some cases, we've held such retreats for over a thousand people. You can make your presentation via satellite, or hold "town hall" meetings department by department. Two things are important. First: the method of communication must be different enough to distinguish this process from everything else that's going on in your organization. Second: the method of communication must be two-way; it must allow for discussion. Other methods of two-way communication include:
  - creating a newsletter with response columns focusing on the challenges of change specific to the program;
  - making the change contingent on communication by making consultation part of the pre-change process, with group brainstorming sessions;

- letting your customers voice their needs directly. Let them demonstrate the need for change using fax-back quality surveys or "service wish lists."

• Create opportunities for showing people in the organization how the company's pain affects them personally. Make everyone aware of the risks of not changing by proving that the dangers are there. Use stories from the business press to illustrate your points in conjunction with your own projections. Examples bring the information to life. Show your administrators, executives and front-line workers how others in their fields are taking new approaches, teaching a little history. Combat the feeling that "tradition's being messed with" by illustrating how the history of the company is all about change, and show how those changes have led to success.

• Offer hope; demonstrate the benefits of making the change. Spare no detail. Include decor, itineraries, working methods, tools and working relationships.

The organization feels pain, but management doesn't.

• Cry "Ouch!" If you're not in the leadership, but clearly see pain current or looming, share this knowledge. Document your reasons for concern as specifically as possible (cite intuitive reasons as well as quantifiable ones). State your case to a senior sponsor who can reach the leadership if you are not in a position to do so.

- Keep stating your case to anyone who will listen. Call them. Talk to them in the cafeteria lineup. Ask them for a meeting. Initiate a discussion on E-mail, or in the company newsletter, or through voice-mail. Everyone should know what you think.

- Unveil the naked truth by publishing pain. The front-line worker should have as much knowledge about why change is necessary as his or her manager, so don't hold back or you'll have your employees wasting their energies on trying to figure out "why" instead of "how" change will occur. Report on it.

- Make a presentation to senior people. Sometimes we've found that it's good to make this presentation to a newly-appointed executive; that person has less ego invested in "the way things are done around here."

You and the organization feel pain, but your management team doesn't.
- Communicate and persuade. As the leader, you must hold the mirror; help your team members reflect on the situation. Jolt them as necessary.

- Get the team out of the comfort of the office. Disorient them by having the meeting somewhere unusual. Give them enough time at the meeting that they must go past their usual defenses. And the "field" trips should be aimed at putting them in direct contact with the realities of the daily lives of the people they work with. Take them for a subway ride. Take them to the supermarket. Take them on tour of the factory or the workplace of a supplier or client. Dare them to switch places with their secretaries for a day.

- Show them where the trip will take them: If they are inspired and buy into the goal, they will see the need for change.

- Advertise the goal. Put it on the stationery, on the electronic bulletin boards, at the front gate. The goal must be powerful to counteract the culture that's keeping your organization static.

- If all else fails, you may have to replace the team or part of it.

No one feels pain.
- If your company is feeling no pain then it's lacking nerves. It's practicing deliberate blindness. If this is the case, an external source must push you toward

change. Think about your position with respect to each of these elements:

- your competition: how is it changing? How are you responding?
- industry watchdogs: what's the buzz? Are you in tune with the developing pictures of the future of your industry?
- shareholders: why are they *your* shareholders? Are you giving them enough reason to remain your shareholders?
- customers: why do your clients buy from you? Are you adding to their list of reasons?
- industry analysts: what are the numbers revealing about your success compared to that of your competitors? What about other related markets?
- consultants: are you seeking perspective on the position of your company?

We've seen a lot of "smug" organizations. That smugness is usually a serious signal for change.

Still no pain? You've lost interest and it may be time to look for another job.

"Leaders must build communities inside their corporation and live with communities outside their corporation. This is not inefficient; it is the way of the world that is going to be required in the global economy."

MANUEL ARANGO, PRESIDENT, GRUPO CONCORDE S.A. DE C.V.

CHAPTER TWO

What Needs to Change?

The eternal triangle

·

What does your organization believe, *really?*

·

It's better in groups

·

Response ability

Take Your Wish List — and Burn It

"We need to fire Howard Bonmonth and hire a really good bagpiper." Ah . . . it was the early days: Dr. Marti Smye was blowing the damp off her doctorate and advising her first Leaders of Industry on how to make great leaps forward.

"Fire Howard Bonmonth and hire a really good bagpiper." It was written right there: the first response I'd gotten from the first employee survey we'd taken at a large resources company.

Right: for this I'd slaved through all those years of university. For this Doris and Marty (Senior) of Salineville, Ohio, had worked the soil and made the

Necessary Sacrifices. For this my brother Marty (it's what you could call a close family) had taught me how to stay up all night to finish a paper. For this.

Maybe, I thought, if I thoroughly analyzed the situation, I could make a case for this large resources company to set itself on the road to the future by sacrificing, as its first act in its new era, one Howard Bonmonth and directing the necessary monies into the employment of a really good bagpiper. It could be a symbolic act — an unfettering of the company from its traditions and mythologies. After all, highly-trained industrial psychologists are taught to have a minimum of preconceptions in dealing with disparate corporate cultures. As a rational and educated consultant, I had to take firing Howie and hiring the piper as an option.

As a leader — of a company, a section, a division or a branch — you have a problem. You need to decide what has to change. Because you purchased this book and have put some thought into the subject — you've probably already started a wish list. And you feel passionate about it.

Burn that list. By the time your organization has started to change, it will be out of date anyway. And there may be more interesting ideas that come up when you canvass everyone in the organization. Treat suggestions with an open mind—even ones about bagpipers.

All the same, don't fire Howard yet. Establish a common ground which will let you discover what are the motivations of some of your people for recruiting a bagpiper.*

A Change Model

Models are a way of condensing the big picture, and can help prevent a leader from getting bogged down in details as he or she guides change. To understand the processes underlying change, we use a model based on the Greek symbol, delta, to represent change as a triangle (see Figure 1). Take a photocopy of this model. Put it up where you can see it from where you work. Better yet, make two copies, and put the other one up where you'll see it every day at home.

The change triangle helps to identify key issues in any organization's change strategy. The three key issues are organization, groups and individuals. Change must be successfully implemented at every one of these three levels, or your organization's new strategy is doomed to failure. And people issues — buy-in, commitment, beliefs — lie at the heart of each of these three levels.

---

*It isn't fair for me to leave you hanging. In this highly-disguised case history, we retrained and redirected Mr. Bonmonth. We also put a jukebox on the factory floor.

Figure 1 — The Change Triangle[1]

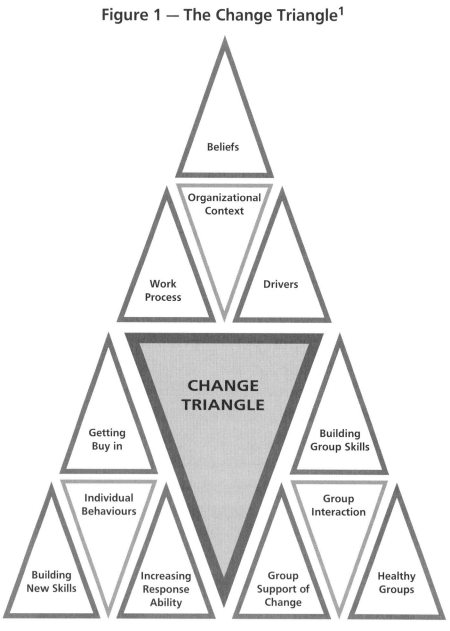

[1] Copyright People Tech Consulting Inc.

What Must Change at the Organizational Level

After 16 years and hundreds of cases, we've learned that in every organization, there are three areas to master: beliefs, performance drivers and work process.

Beliefs

A belief system includes your organization's vision and values; business purpose and strategy; strengths and weaknesses; and a recognition of who matters, and how much. That's the psychologist in me talking; let's make things simpler.

Organizations have belief systems. This belief system is evident in the company's vision statement, business strategies and core competencies. What do people believe the organization can and cannot do? Who is perceived as important? (for example, if technical or engineering staff are more highly regarded than marketing staff, it is an indication of where the organization believes its real strength lies.) Who do people do things for? If people do things for the boss before they do things for the customer, that is another message about beliefs.

As a leader, your job is to help create a belief system that is consistent with the dreams and direction of the organization. If the beliefs are negative, evaluating and addressing the reasons for cynicism will be at the heart of your change platform. You have to foster organizational confidence before you can harness it.

If you understand your company's belief system, you can mobilize it and turn the organization in new and daring directions. One of our clients tried it and won. This company had thought it was successful; it consistently achieved 15% return on sales. The staff knew that they were doing a good job; their mantra for success was "Success equals 15%." One day, the world tilted: the shareholders asked for a 20% return. Overnight, high achievers became underachievers. Challenged and motivated, the staff were eager to restore success, to re-establish that successful belief system. They discovered new ways of working and achieved the extra 5%.

The lesson? Challenging belief systems means results. It also means resistance, which must be recognized and addressed. But a well-defined organizational vision tends to forestall the need for crisis management, and allows changes to be effected smoothly. If your organization's present belief system is not working or is out of date, alter it. Rewrite the way the employees see the company.

Performance Drivers
To reinforce the belief system, an organization needs to have a system of measurement in place. At People Tech we call these "the performance drivers." They provide feedback, targets and incentives. Performance drivers include goals such as sales and volume increases; key

results; reporting systems; and reward systems. If you have a new vision, or change direction without changing performance drivers, the effect is similar to sending employees the wrong way down a one-way street: they are going to be confused and collide with one another. New performance drivers highlight the benefits of change on our lives by tying day-to-day actions to the overall vision. Workers must be able to see how their changed behavior will result in a measurable, and therefore rewardable, difference.

One client of ours wanted to improve cash flow by getting customer accounts paid faster. The sales force, however, was not committed to this goal; since they were paid a set commission regardless of when bills were paid, their performance was driven by that system. Once management varied the commissions, and rewarded salespeople for motivating accounts to pay more quickly, receivables flowed in swiftly. The performance drivers had to match the situation in order for the objective to be reached. Too many firms ask their people to accept change, but offer no incentive for doing so.

Work Process

The management style of the 1980s was vertical; departments worked independently to achieve narrowly defined goals. The bottom line dictated that the sales department should sell more, the production department should increase speed of output, the finance department should achieve better margins and then all would be sweetness and light. However in the 1980s we learned painfully that customers are not interested in our bottom line. They want improved product, price and service levels. These customer demands exposed several weaknesses in the traditional 1980s-style organization:

- It is slow to respond.
- It smothers individual talent.
- Work gets duplicated.
- There is little cooperation between departments.
- It is deaf to the customer.

The problem with vertical management is that in reality, no department functions independently. The workload typically involves many departments. When you go to the hospital for surgery, each professional there has a vertical specialty: the anesthetist puts you to sleep, the surgeon operates, the nurse handles the tools, the administration gives you the bill. However, you do expect the specialists to coordinate themselves and remove your gall bladder *after* you are unconscious. Customers expect the same coordination of efforts from organizations.

Another problem arising in work process can be found in Elliott Jaques' concept of time horizons. Organizations are structured hierarchically because task-time horizons differ, and individual accountability and compensation are based on these tasks. Line staff typically perform tasks that have a time horizon of a few hours or a few days. Supervisors and managers may have a task-time horizon of several weeks or months (preparing work schedules, developing budgets, for example). At the highest level, senior executives have task-time horizons that may span years (developing strategic plans, for example). In many organizations these distinctions become confused. People may be operating at levels that are above or below the level at which they should be performing. For example, senior executives may spend most of their time on operational tasks when they should be focusing on their longer-term activities, whereas supervisors may be involved in tasks that their managers should be doing, at the expense of managing their own people.

Flattening the organization can avoid duplication of effort and turf wars. The fewer boundaries there are in an organization, the fewer lives there are to step on — or over.

"You have to think with your head and your heart. If you separate the two, you are no longer a business person. If you separate heart and mind, you will undoubtedly make a bad decision."

SYLVANO (SYL) GHIRARDI, GROUP VICE-PRESIDENT,

APPLIED SCIENCE & MANUFACTURING TECHNOLOGY

CIBA VISION GROUP MANAGEMENT

MANAGEMENT TIP:

*Here are some ideas to get your organization
ready for change*

BELIEFS

· Recognize the existing mental models — the imagined set of boundaries operating in your organization. What are the implicit assumptions your organization has operated under in the past? Is there a gap between these and today's business realities? What counterproductive actions do these assumptions generate? Which assumptions could be more appropriate, given the changes you are trying to create?

· Help employees understand the larger context of the business — the external forces changing the business as well as the consequences of employees' actions on the whole organization.

· Encourage experimentation and reflection. Adults change when they have the opportunity to try out new actions, observe the results, reflect and try again. Learning to "think about thinking" is key to changing assumptions and behavior.

PERFORMANCE DRIVERS

· Align your performance drivers with your change. Link individual targets by demonstrating causality (if you do this, I can do that, and together we'll achieve this).

Wherever possible, quantify the terms of success (get ten leads a month, elicit three customer compliments a day, institute one process improvement a month, etc.).

WORK PROCESS

· Elliott Jaques argues that the problem of many organizations is that people are unclear about what they are accountable for achieving. This uncertainty leads to overlaps of responsibilities and lack of clarity in roles throughout the organization. If employees understand what they are ultimately accountable for, many of the problems with inefficient work processes resolve themselves. To address this issue, define the purpose of key jobs in your organization (ask, "Why does this job exist?"). Who are the jobs' key customers and what are the customers' expectations? How is job success measured? What are the core competencies required to meet customer expectations?

What Must Change at the Group Level

Teamwork is the new norm. This reality involves new challenges for employee interaction: how we regard each other and how we cooperate. The new heroes are those who know how to mobilize the energy of the groups they work in. When humans work together, synergy, that process of making the whole greater than the sum of the parts, is essential. You will need to know how to build group skills, foster healthy groups and ensure group support of change.

> "To overcome pockets of resistance, I created a core group of 24 section and department heads. They became part of the strategy and bought into it; they then passed their commitment down to their subordinates. They were able to counter resistance with one-on-one discussions. Peer pressure alone isn't enough, though; we had to be vigilant, identify problems before they started, and handle them sensitively."
>
> MAX STREBEL, PRESIDENT AND CEO, UNION BANK OF SWITZERLAND

Building Group Skills

It is natural to feel that we work best with people we know. Cooperating with others outside that circle creates tension. They don't speak our language. They have different priorities. They don't understand our jobs — and we don't understand theirs. Because of these tensions it's important to help people to step out of their comfort zone and to enable them to function as one large group.

Building team skills is an essential area because, for true alignment of beliefs, performance drivers and work processes, the organization must move in unison. For example, Xerox Corporation is for many a model of service quality. They even sell their "Quality System" to other companies. One of the components that has made the system a success is Xerox's common language of problem-solving. The system, the methodology and the language used in all teams across the Xerox Corporation are the same. This creates a common bond and heightens efficiency when people are working together. A common language is required to create a unique organization that can move in unison.

What are the characteristics of high-performing teams? They:

- establish ground rules of how the team will work;
- decide important issues by consensus;
- encourage input from all team members;
- continually reflect upon and evaluate the quality of their work;
- keep the team focused on results;
- recognize the contribution of each team member;
- encourage personal growth and support.

At AT&T, we worked with a pilot team of people from various functions focused on sales and service for a particular product. At first there was resistance in these groups, as engineers started working alongside sales staff. That initial resistance arose because people were not working beside "their own type," who shared the same experience, language and skill sets. Working with the entire group we identified the behaviors that they felt would be required for a fully functioning, healthy and supportive team. On the basis of these behaviors, we designed a diagnostic tool to measure the contribution each individual made to the team.

As you can imagine, the initial reaction to the measurement was fear and suspicion. We pressed on because our belief was that if new behaviors could be instilled, then the performance of the team would be increased and the bottom-line goals would be met. Each individual received a confidential performance appraisal on a quarterly basis. Over time, the team became more successful and the feedback became more welcome, because success and support are addictive. This group then sold this technique to other teams within AT&T as a way of improving performance.

The appraisals showed the group exactly how individual efforts contributed to their overall success. They made the power of these efforts tangible and eventually instilled a sense of control and confidence in the group. What they achieved became more noticeable, further feeding this confidence in their ability to make a difference. It made them feel a little less lonely in the middle.

Healthy Groups

Teamwork alone isn't enough; change demands a certain type of teamwork. Teams can promote change — or kill it.

It is common for teams to have a "them versus us" point of view; common, perhaps, but it means certain death to team systems. Healthy groups depend on leveling barriers and eliminating stereotypes. Mutual respect and understanding will allow room for growth, and facilitate an environment for the accomplishment of the impossible. You can achieve this environment through a number of means.

Try these techniques:
- Give individuals "day passes" they can use to spend a day sitting in on another team.
- Make every team's business everybody's business. Establish a monthly question sheet that circulates queries teams have about other teams.
- Create partnering opportunities between teams by giving them projects that require them to work together toward a common goal.

Arriving at one client site recently, we found two departments at odds. The manufacturing organization insisted that all company employees should have their work time formally documented to improve record-keeping. Sales, of course, objected — how can salespeople be expected to punch a clock? These groups failed to recognize or understand each other's jobs and needs. Now they are working to find a solution, by "walking a mile in the other person's shoes."

"When I first arrived in Belgium, the company was a
product of the merger of two companies as different as
day and night. It wasn't working. I tried to understand
what went wrong and I realized no one had built a
common culture or vision; this was just two large
companies thrown together, underperforming, going
nowhere. We set up a number of task forces with input
from our top 60 people. The task forces identified the
problems, not me. They had to work together to identify
the problem, then solve it. They had to understand what
was wrong, and how to fix it. The teams owned it
completely. If I had done it top-down, it would have
taken five years. This way, it took only 18 months
and it's still going on."

RON TOMLINSON, GENERAL MANAGER, KRAFT JACOB SUCHARD

Let me just clarify my meaning here: a team is a
group that works together. Groups themselves do not necessarily constitute teams. Individual performance on a
sports team is a vital ingredient of success — but unless
the team is set up to enhance individual performance, it
is just a group of individuals working hard, and sometimes against each other in an effort geared more toward
protecting their reputations than toward winning the
game. Teams look for ways to make the best use of each
individual's strengths. It is through the examination of
each team-member's strengths that the team can best

learn to work together. And when a team is determined to do that, it is ready to look for creative ways of working together to meet the demands of their internal and external clients.

Reaching this level of team confidence requires some bravery and a little patience. Any new venture will go through — and should go through — some chaos before an order of sorts emerges (and of course the order should be changed from time to time, to re-mine the talents of its members).

Try this: create a team to work on a particular project. Purposefully do *not* lay out the roles of the team members. Instead, provide the team with a critical path that charts when the larger aspects of the project are to be completed. Tell the team members to use their first week to establish a detailed plan for the project, complete with work assignments, resource requirements and suggestions for addressing any foreseen challenges or expenses presented by the project. Tell them that the plan shouldn't be more than five pages long, and that you want a list of any contacts they used in developing the plan. Then give them some paper, a computer, some phones and some space and see what they come up with.

Creative team approaches are born out of a study of the world at large and a willingness to try something new. "Best practices" are not just those within your industry in your region, but are ideally drawn from books, magazines, television, movies, travel, university, brochures, radio, music, conversations, studies, reports, comparisons, computers — general observation. The executive team becomes, in effect, an ongoing scanning machine, and one that keeps prodding for more input.

Group Support of Change

The purpose of building team skills and ensuring that groups are healthy is to use those groups to get the organization to move toward change. We join diet centers in order to work together to lose weight. We work out at the gym and share the pains and the gains with fellow members. In fact, we all use other people in many ways to achieve common goals. And by working in groups we not only make better decisions and create more innovative solutions, but we also have more fun and can get the support as we move to the highs and lows of the changes ahead of us.

"Business is still treating workers as we did in 1910 — 'shut up kid and do your job.' Management must change its attitude towards what its people resource is, and what it should be doing; meetings are not something you do, it's how you run the business."

RON COMPTON, PRESIDENT AND CEO,

AETNA LIFE & CASUALTY COMPANY

What Must Change at the Level of the Individual

Individual behaviors are the litmus test for meeting change objectives. Three ways to influence individual behavior are by gaining buy-in, increasing "response ability" and building new skills.

Gaining Buy-In

There can be no change until individual employees agree that proposed changes are necessary and will be effective.

Imagine a situation in which you are pressured to provide a yes or no answer. You are not ready to answer, but you have no choice; you must respond.

Now step back. How are you feeling? Hesitation, uncertainty and frustration will all be on your list of emotions. Resistance is our way of buying time so that we can work through the implications of change.

Now imagine being asked to provide input into the decision-making process. Your pre-decision involvement puts you in touch with the decision details. When the decision is made, your concerns have been addressed. You help people say yes to change by involving them in the process of change.

Remember that every individual's perspective on the business affects how they perceive the case that you present to them. Input should not be accepted in a vacuum but with a thorough understanding of "where it's coming from." Leaders should seek to enhance and demonstrate this understanding.

MANAGEMENT TIP:

Make the case for change one person at a time

It is important to speak to an individual in the language of what is important to him or her.

- For executives, consider the long-term purpose of the change.
- For managers, assess the operational impact of the change.
- For the front line, focus on the job satisfaction and security that will result from the change.

Increasing Response Ability

In order for us to make the changes we want, to do their jobs in a new way and to pass decision-making down to the lowest level in the organization, we need to give them the power. To some this translates into "empowerment" — quite possibly the most overused word and underused practice in business today.

We prefer to use the term "response ability" — giving

people the ability to respond. We need to give them what's necessary — technology, skills or information — so that they are able to meet the new demands of their jobs.

Too often these days, leaders hope to unleash the potential of people by telling them what to think. Any leader who tries that tactic has failed. At any level in the organization people are capable of making judgments, meeting customer needs and to coming up with new ideas — if they have the same information base and knowledge as those who previously made those decisions.

In the information age knowledge is no longer the exclusive perquisite of the highly educated or the highly tenured. Enormous libraries of information are available to anyone from a desktop. Computers, telephones, televisions, VCRs and tape machines are all the tools anyone needs to access several lifetimes of knowledge — and this wealth of information can all be had for less than the cost of a university education. A university degree is no trivial achievement, but is not the only measure of a worker's ability to do the job he or she's been assigned (it is the thinking process that we learn at university, not necessarily the knowledge base).

"Response ability" calls for commitment from both worker and leader. I have a true story which drives home the point. A group of insurance employees raised concerns about how outdated their policy manual was, and how that made it hard for them to give answers to their claims customers. During the initiation of a major change, they told the CEO their concerns on one of his visits. He responded by immediately tearing the manual in two. Shocked, the employees asked, "What will we do without a policy manual?" He replied, "You will just have to think." This implies a two-way commitment. On the one hand, the CEO was demonstrating emphatically the confidence that he had in his staff to live by their new values. On the other hand, he needed to provide them with the ability to respond by giving them the new skills and the *information data base* (as distinct from the *policy manual*) to serve customers more effectively. In this instance, the data base was eventually provided.

> "The way to help individuals manage change is to let people know everything. People are generally adaptable, are of goodwill, and want to contribute. Most people can cope with just about anything, if they know why. They become hostile and resistant when they don't know everything, or perceive that they don't know."
>
> ANNE FAWCETT, MANAGING PARTNER, THE CALDWELL PARTNERS INTERNATIONAL

Building New Skills

When new skills are required, the natural first response is to feel awkward and uncomfortable. If you've ever been forced to write with the wrong hand due to an injury, you'll know the feeling. While we are learning new skills, it is difficult to accept mistakes, yet temporary failures are a normal part of learning. Organizations must recognize this dichotomy and assist people in getting past the discomfort onto a new skill level. This requires allowing people to make mistakes . . . for a time. Let them explore new avenues of personal ability. There are many benefits to the organization in this approach: the more skills an employee can master, the better a resource the employee is for the firm. Flexibility and adaptability are enhanced and employees can take their knowledge with them to new teams.

Building new skills calls for confidence. We believe that corporations have a responsibility to promote this sense of internal confidence in their workers, as opposed to yesterday's promises of lifetime employment. When we look back at the industrial age, we will realize that we have created legions of dependent employees. We have told them that if they came to work and did as they were told, life would be good. As we now realize that this model will not work for us in the information age, we have been downsizing our corporations and throwing our employees to the wolves. We cannot provide security for our employees — the type of security that says "you will always have a job here." But we can provide the skills to help them survive. The only way to do this is to create a continuous-learning culture. People will take on new tasks and new jobs because they learn new skills and will therefore have more skills to offer at their next job and, potentially, at their next company.

Part of this process must be directed toward the individual. Companies can help people to examine their own belief systems, can raise their self-esteem and encourage them to believe they can walk over hot coals. Security comes from within, but today's leaders have a responsibility to help individuals through this transition period from dependency to independence.

Imagine a world of individuals who believe in themselves, understand their strengths and weaknesses and always feel as if they are working for themselves! Of course, this implies a new social contract with our employees, but it also means that people will stay in their jobs because it serves their purpose to do the job well. To naysayers this may seem idealistic, but for us to compete in the global economy, it is absolutely essential.

"You have to be sensitive to individual concerns, and help them recognize that the organization is different. Get them individually involved in the early process, skunkworks, forming teams, getting ideas and concerns on the table. Teach them a process to deal with change, educate your people, and equip them with tools to solve problems."

TOM McKENNA, PRESIDENT AND CEO, MOORMAN MANUFACTURING COMPANY

CHAPTER THREE

Are We Ready for Change?

The enemy: complacency

·

Change readiness — test yourself

·

Overcoming resistance

·

Three types of motivation

·

Making the case for change

"We're Almost Perfect Now"

In 1899, the United States patent office almost decided to close down. It was their view that everything that could be invented *had* been invented. Life was as perfect as it would get.

There are a lot of companies that have decided the same thing. After all, when a company's had the caliber of management *they've* had for *as long* as they've had it, how could things be less than perfect?

Understandably, their employees usually think the same thing.

You don't have to be a management consultant to spot these symptoms:

- You know you're dealing with the almost perfect company when you phone them and get shunted around on voice-mail for 20 minutes. They've got the perfect telephone system — for their management. It must be perfect, otherwise they'd change it.
- You know you're dealing with the almost perfect company when you find the warranty is worthless. It has attained the kind of perfection you get when a document is customer-proof. It must be perfect, otherwise they'd change it.
- You know you're dealing with the almost perfect company when the person behind the counter says, "We can't do that." Their policy must be perfect, otherwise they'd change it.

Take a moment: you could probably think of a few more examples. Then think of the "perfect" qualities of your company that consumers trip over. And think about why your people aren't telling you to change them.

How Ready Are You for Change?

Ask yourself these questions — and be brutally honest in your answers.

- Do most of the people in my organization, and particularly senior management, understand the need for change?

- Do I have a clear vision of what our organization needs to become?
- Do we have a leadership team that shares a vision of change, and a commitment to it?
- Have we identified the barriers to change, and the opportunities for it in our organization?
- Have we identified the barriers to and opportunities for change in our organization?
- Do we have a clear, logical plan that reflects the organization's ability to change?
- Have we established milestones and measures of success, and do we have a way to keep track of what we learn?
- Have we created incentives and systems that will move us closer to our vision?

If you answered no to two or more questions, your organization's ability to implement change effectively is questionable. You may want to examine closely the implications of undertaking a major initiative that may not deliver the expected benefits.

Involving Your People in the Decision to Change
As we said before, getting people to say yes to change means involving them in the decision to make change.

Consider the following factors when designing a plan to initiate a change.

"Vision is not just a sign on the wall. You have to work
it through the organization. You have to overcome
cynicism, and work long and hard with dedication.
I would say I have spent about 30 to 40% of my
personal time on this change management process."

RON TOMLINSON, GENERAL MANAGER, KRAFT JACOB SUCHARD

Resistance

A free exchange of information and discussion about
change is key to ensuring minimal resistance to your
initiatives. Also key is a clear understanding of how
resistance is born.

WHY PEOPLE DON'T DO "IT"

· They don't know why they should do it.
· They don't know how to do it.
· They don't know what they are supposed to do.
· They think your way won't work
· They think their way is better.
· They think something else is more important.
· There is no positive consequence to them for doing it.
· They think they are doing it but they aren't.
· They are rewarded for not doing it.
· There are obstacles beyond their control.
· They are punished for doing what they are
supposed to do.

· They anticipate a negative consequence for
doing it.
· There is no negative consequence to them
for poor performance.
· Their personal limits prevent them from performing.
· They have personal problems.
· No one could do it.

FERDINAND FOURNIES, 1988

MANAGEMENT TIP:

Understanding resistance

Resistance is actually healthy; try not to react against it defensively. It is good for you: it makes you check your assumptions. It forces you to clarify what you are doing. You must always probe the objections to find the real reason for resistance; usually, it comes down to personal fear. As the leader, you must take the time to understand resistance; you may have to come at it from several different angles before it is conquered. You must understand what the objector is feeling, as well as thinking.

Three Types of Motivation

We need to be aware that, in contemplating change, most people have one of three motivations: safety — the need to be cared for and nurtured; interest — the need to learn and have continuing excitement and challenge; and rationality — the need for logical, analytical reasoning. Each type of motivation needs a change process that speaks to it. The trick is for the CEO to be able to engage in multipurpose communications that will satisfy all three.

In order to address all three motivations, the leader will need to design change processes to accommodate each one. This implies more than just calling everyone into a room together. Understanding the three motivations can also help a leader understand what is behind resistance, by listening for what seems to be important to a person or group.

Type of motivation	Where we are	What is the pain	How to stop the pain
Safety	We're in trouble	I'm feeling insecure about my job	Show me that I can contribute
Interest	We haven't done anything new in years around here	I'm bored	Engage in a variety of experiments
Rational	We're ten points behind the competition	Things don't add up	Make a plan

Gain Shared Agreement and Understanding

Here are some techniques for making the case for change:

- *Use cold, hard facts to give your people a whack alongside the head.* Find those two or three key facts which — if extrapolated over a five-year to ten-year period would be devastating to your organization, especially compared to what the competition's doing or to what other industries are doing. Example: take your declining margins and project them seven years ahead. Example: take the size of your workforce and project it. Example: project future service standards from the gains you've made in the past five years.

- *Bring predictions and forecasts into the present — and don't let people explain them away.* You'll get some discomfiting reactions from sharing the facts. Your people will say things like "That's too scary to happen" and "Those figures are just part of a cycle that'll pass." Your reaction? Ask "What would you do if the scenario I've given you has even a 50% chance of happening?" and "What if it isn't a cycle?" Be provocative. Get people to put together their own scenarios right at the meeting. You may not end up with an accurate prediction of the future — but you will be on the way to sharing agreement on why change is needed.

- *Make the facts meaningful.* Shake the discussion loose with questions like "What would the customers say if they knew this?" and "What would the stockholders' reactions be?" Illustrate the reporting of facts with case studies and testimonials to humanize figures or reports.

- *Make the implications personal.* Say things like "Here's what that scenario is going to do to me" — and ask questions like "What's it going to do to you?"

- *Remind everyone that the one option that is not available is staying the same.* Above all, creating a commitment to making change involves defining the change strategy concept. Once you understand the case, the status quo is no longer viable. There is sadness in letting go a cherished belief system. Try to provide an opportunity for relinquishing the status quo at a personal level: ritualize it; create a garbage bin or fire. Define the pain implications of the status quo versus the change; combat misperceptions about pain amongst the workforce.

- *Conduct a senior group retreat.* Organizations have been doing this for years, because it works. You can make it work even better if it's not a traditional retreat. Why not hold it in Cody, Wyoming, instead of Boca, Florida? After all there's not a lot to do in Cody except stick to the subject and talk it out until you get agreement.

- *Be open in sharing the underlying values of your organization and its leadership.* I'm not talking about shared goals — I'm talking about shared values. If your people don't share the value of a team approach or the value of other people's ideas, you're losing. How do you get at what those values are? Read on.

What Am I Letting Myself In For?

CHAPTER FOUR

Getting Started

"Bigger whiteboards"

·

Corporate foreplay

·

Four types of change management

·

Strategic planning and strategic deciding

·

New ways of convincing your organization to change

Bigger Whiteboards: Most Important

I've been to more strategy meetings than you have. It's my job.

I have to tell you that some of these meetings are very strange. They often bung up in jargon clog. The conversation around the table goes something like this:

"Well, Ted, that's not really a strategy. It's a tactic, and tactics are the instruments of strategy."

"And we can't have the tactics before we do the mission statement."

"But you have to realize, Duane, that the mission statement can't go before we draft the values statement."

"But, in and of itself, the values statement *is*, de facto, a strategy, isn't it, Edna?"

"It's an *objective*. Which means it goes before the strategy. But it's necessarily preceded by . . ."

I'm about to get into a little jargon clog myself in this chapter — but just a little. This chapter talks about the difference between strategic planning and strategic deciding. The deciding alternative is better than the planning alternative because it involves more people.

> "I never knew how personal the change would be.
> It's not easy; it's a roller coaster experience,
> but it makes you stronger. I have moved from being
> a solid supporter of the need for change intellectually,
> to recognizing it deeply, to feeling that it is the most
> important thing to think about and feel and be
> constantly aware of. Moving from the role of solid
> supporter to champion is very scary, but change
> won't happen unless someone does this. The thing to
> watch for is that as a leader you have struggled a
> long time thinking and feeling about the need for
> change, but you must recognize that others have not
> had that timeline. You start to think it's obvious, you
> expect everyone to get it, but you must realize
> that you are ahead of people and you have
> to give them time to catch up."
>
> MARY ANN CHAMPLIN, SENIOR VICE-PRESIDENT
>
> AETNA HUMAN RESOURCES, AETNA LIFE & CASUALTY COMPANY

Involving more people is good for a very practical reason. If you involve more people, you're going to have to reach out to the sales guy in Arkansas and the production planner from France. These are people who neither by instinct nor by inclination want to mess with jargon clog. Instead they say things like "These new gimbels of the 74A don't do diddley and my customers want them fixed," and "When are you going to let me know what you're doing so I can get my people working on it?"

Those are the kinds of questions that it's difficult for someone in a power suit to write down on the whiteboard during the strategy symposium. The secret is to get a bigger whiteboard — or whatever it takes to get more of your people involved in the process.

You've decided why your organization needs to change, what to change and whether you're ready for those changes. Now comes the tough part. Your next steps are to announce the change and begin implementation. These steps are tough. Most companies never get beyond announcing change. They wallow in the tasks of coming up with a slogan such as "Tomorrow's Organization TODAY!!" and coloring the boxes on the organization charts in pastels instead of primary colors . . . and then the whole effort dribbles to a stop. Something like last year's Ultimate Exercise Course.

Let's consider realities.

For some organizations — those in a merger situation, for example — these steps will be compressed and dramatic. Others are looking at the change of a culture over a five- to seven-year period.

What we've found out at People Tech is that, in both situations, most organizations don't think in advance about how they are initiating their change agenda, or communicating it, or implementing it. But just as in proposing marriage — or divorce — or a Saturday night interlude between two systems analysts — some techniques are more effective than others. A marriage proposal from someone who hasn't done a little romancing first doesn't work; there should be, uh, a *little* foreplay *before*. In a divorce from an abusive partner, it's better if your lawyer writes a note and you move out over the weekend. If a marriage to a good friend is ending, it's better to seek counseling together to bring closure and ensure that mutual respect remains. A Saturday night interlude? It depends entirely on the particular systems analysts involved.

Implementing change in organizations is no different from these situations. Sometimes we don't have much choice. But even when our organizational choices are limited, we need to think about the process: what we are doing and the impact it will have on people. We should use the many methods of communication available to us, and anticipate their questions. We must ensure that we spend time, when time is required. We must engage all of the leaders in the communications efforts, and ensure a consistency of message, a consistency of behavior. And we have to go beyond this; for if we don't understand the pain that will be experienced in the implementation of change, we will not be able to provide the support that the organization requires.

We make the pain easier by identifying certain styles of change management, so that you can choose one that's right for your organization. By defining the style, you're taking a positive step toward taking control of the change process, and you can understand better who needs to participate, and how long you need to make change work. Mind you, just as in marriage, divorce or the dialectic delicacies of the tryst, you have to remember that you're dealing with humans. And that one of them is you.

> **"Some companies change their vision to meet what's in front of them; they should change what's in front of them to fit the vision."**
>
> F. PETER CUNEO, PRESIDENT & CEO, REMINGTON PRODUCTS COMPANY

The Four Types of Change Management

There are four models for change management: top-down, cascade, networked and cloning (see Figure 2). Each relies on management to build a commitment to change in the workplace, but in different ways. There is

Figure 2 — The Four Types of Change Management

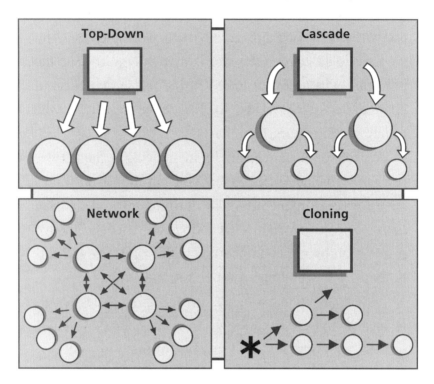

no such thing as a "one size fits all" approach. What works well for one company may produce disastrous results for another. The solution at IBM ain't the solution at Apple.

- The first, and traditional, model for change management is *top-down*. The leader decides on the nature of the restructuring, and issues (in the words of Captain Picard of the *Enterprise*) an edict to "make it so." There is little discussion or involvement at any other level, except in simple execution. In these days of empowered workforces and flattening hierarchies, it's easy to dismiss the top-down approach. If used wisely, however, it will continue to have a place when circumstances — such as a corporate crisis or a sudden merger — demand urgent, sweeping actions. The merger of a subsidiary of General Foods with a major former competitor was the result of a swift decision by senior management. But it was General Foods' management's commitment to post-merger employee communications and involvement which assured long-term success.

- In the *cascade* or *leader-led* approach, managers promote new behavior through their own example. This type of change management is particularly appropriate when a deep-rooted organizational culture clings to "old ways" because they have served the company well in the past. Pepsi-Cola International, a thriving enterprise that has expanded operations in recent years, faced such a challenge when it moved to gain greater control over its retail trade. Each level of management has always looked to the next one up to set expectations at Pepsi. Because of that long-standing culture, they couldn't mandate change from one level to the next without showing personal commitment. Beginning with the president, one tier of management coached the next tier, which in turn coached another, and so on through the ranks, much like a cascading fountain of champagne glasses.

- The third model of change management is that of a *network*. In contrast with the cascade model, the networked approach brings together highly capable "opinion leaders" from all areas of the company to form a kind of corporate SWAT team, empowered to cut through red tape, to drive a business agenda forward and to pump up performance. Skills rather than titles determine who takes part; the networks transcend the boundaries of traditional hierarchies and give change credibility in the eyes of workers. The Royal Bank of Canada has instituted management reforms based on networks. With 54,000 employees distributed worldwide, the challenge of rolling out change consistently was and is considerable. One answer was to turn all of the bank's area managers into a network — a close-knit group that routinely shares best practices, learns from each other's problems and works together to understand the business more deeply. Many organizations favor networks as an alternative to full-scale restructuring, and with good reason: networked change can diffuse deeply entrenched resistance to new practices.

- The fourth model of change management has been described by Michael Beer; I refer to this as the *cloning model*. In this model you begin change in one part of the organization and learn about the impact it has on the organization and people. Then you make revisions, create a wider enthusiasm and encourage the spread of this model to other parts of the organization. Typically, this pilot approach is effective when you are unsure of the impact of change on the organization, how things will be accomplished or when there may be a natural resistance to the change.

You start in a department or division where people are change-ready. There is also an additional criteria: the department must be respected by the rest of the company. In other words, you set up your change shop in a place where it is most likely to succeed — and then roll the idea out. This model is possibly the slowest implementation strategy. But it allows for a learning approach and, as Beer notes, has the highest chance for success. Not all corporations can afford the time required by this strategy, and, depending upon the culture of the organization, starting in a single department may create envy or jealousy in other divisions, as well as increased resistance or fear.

Strategic Deciding

Are you involved in strategic planning or strategic deciding?

A strategy is a series of steps that you must take to get you from where you are today to where you need to be tomorrow. It involves defining what business you should be in; it identifies your key goals.

Strategic deciding is distinguished from *strategic planning* by the fact that in the former, leaders involve others in their vision. They get together, they share the pain and they then start to decide and implement strategy. Funny thing: it works.

People Tech was involved with a company that was suddenly losing millions of dollars of profit a month. Almost the first thing we did was to bring about 40 of the organization's leaders together in a room. It was the first time that had ever happened. On the basis of some focus groups held beforehand, and using some other data, we pointed out the pain their people were experiencing. For a hard-nosed company it was a very emotional meeting. It didn't follow a linear process; we went straight from their pain to new ideas for handling it. We went — literally — from tears to innovation. It wasn't smooth or pretty or easy, but within ten weeks the profit loss had been very dramatically reversed.

Strategic deciding includes the opposite forces of analysis and intuition, and reflects both the external and internal environments. Unlike strategic planning, it is not merely the product of a Strength/Weaknesses/Opportunities/Threats analysis. It involves both the market forces and the company itself.

Strategic deciding is also a flexible and dynamic approach to making change *continually*. Change consultant Susan Dunn believes that the best business strategies are never complete. Decisions arise and become hypotheses or experiments which the organization tests; then the results are fed back into the series of steps. Thus strategy, like change, is a never-ending process, and strategic deciding allows for a change within the process itself.

The strategic decision is essentially the decision to change. Conventional management wisdom dictates a lengthy evaluative process to establish the goals of the company, followed by another lengthy process to establish the strategies for realizing those goals and yet another lengthy process to establish ways of measuring the success of the strategies — all before a change is made. I suggest the lengthiness of this pre-change process is totally unnecessary — a waste of time, in fact — as the best-laid plans will run into problems the moment change is initiated. Instead, I submit that the pre-change process should be about preparing the workforce for the small chaos created by change. That's what strategic deciding is about: creating a little chaos —

mixing everyone up — in order to determine what changes need to be made.

Chaos breeds perspective as well as the desire to establish new order. Chaos quickly establishes the need for positive change and focuses energies on developing change *as it is going on.*

Methods of creating chaos include:

- Bringing all department representatives together to "share their pain," as People Tech did in the example. Have them work together to draw up a master list of priorities and ask each executive to choose the top three — not including his or her own suggestion. Have them draw up three suggestions for addressing these priorities. Now divide your executive into groups to fight about their suggestions. Each group picks one suggestion to put forth for implementation. You end up with a rough plan, the details of which will be fought over by implementation teams. If you don't have a team structure, well, that's another way to create chaos. . . .

- Restructuring the company along team lines. Prepare your human resources department to act as an "employment" agency during the period of chaos. Establish general team headings which are different from current department headings. For instance, instead of having a marketing department and a sales department, why not have two marketing/sales teams that both generate ideas for marketing and sales initiatives, and design and implement plans for executing these ideas. Or establish teams under project headings as opposed to function headings. For example, instead of having a team of administrators, you end up with an administrator on every team. Allow staff to apply to work on any team they choose. Now sit back and watch the knowledge base of your organization expand exponentially, and prepare to implement the outpouring of ideas.

• Shuffling executives. Make your managers trade positions with one another for two weeks. They aren't allowed to talk about work with the actual manager of the team or department they've traded with until the two weeks are up. They are each allowed to make three changes during their short tenure.

If you put the right ingredients into the pot, you will get a good stew. It is important to look not for one right answer, but for many right answers over time. While some companies have been successful through opportunistic strategy, we do not think that leaping onto opportunities is the ideal way to proceed. Rather, you should control your destiny by continuing to decipher new facts and information: the leader's role, as Dunn recommends, is to take responsibility for making decisions and *testing* the strategy.

"For organizations to survive in the 90s, they must be fit — lean and capable. They must be fast — bringing more to market successfully. And they must be focused on their strategy."

WAYNE MAILLOUX, PRESIDENT AND CEO,

PEPSI-COLA CANADA LTD.

CHAPTER FIVE

The Stages of Change

Three reasons consultants number everything

·

Ignoring, attending, planning, executing, embedding

·

Dealing with relapse (it's going to happen)

·

The senior management chasm

Why We Put a Number on Everything.

Take a peek at any management book and you'll find that everything is numbered: "The seven steps to personal persuasion," "The four stages of evolving entrepreneurship," "The 1,041 steps to not feeling like a yokel about your whole dumb life."

The numbering comes naturally. It isn't — really — just an attempt to impress you with how organized the author is. It comes out of analyzing activities and finding that, because the activities we're analyzing are *human*, and because humans are, by and large, predictable, the activities can be broken down into stages or steps that are similarly predictable. Being highly trained and extremely

organized, we number those stages: it's part of the predictable behavior of a consultant. In fact, I'm going to
write an article about it: "Eight Stages of Good Consulting." Stage eight is to number the other stages.

In fact, the numbering helps you, the reader. It
prompts you to make sure you haven't missed anything.
It reminds you that the process is evolutionary and doesn't
happen in just one great leap forward. And it allows you
to mark your progress: each little route marker lets you
know how much farther you have to swim through this
part of the swamp.

So there you have it: Three Reasons Why Consultants
Number Everything.

The Five Stages of Change

A Buddhist said that although there is an infinite number
of paths we might choose in life, once we choose a path,
there will be an inevitable pattern and progress in our
experience. Although life's events seem random, many
cultures and thought leaders believe that if we could
stand far enough back, we would see trends and designs
emerging.

It's the same with change. As individuals, we often
perceive change as something external, unplanned,
uncontrollable. Over a five-year period we gain 40
pounds. Our friends (you know who you are) say things
like "Boy, have they changed." From inside it's been very

gradual. It's only when we see an old photograph that we suddenly realize, "Wow, have I larded up." It has "happened to us": it snuck up and stole something from us without our realizing it. But if we stepped back, we would see perhaps the inevitable result of a suddenly recognizable pattern of less exercise and fattier foods.

Nobody forced that pattern on us, though we can always find someone to blame. The truth is that we did it to ourselves, and we can undo it if we wish. If only we can perceive the pattern, we can regain control of the outcome. There are systematic ways of responding (diet, exercise, support groups) to change, once we do see the systemic damage in the pattern.

In business, both research and experience have shown that there is a pattern to change. Individuals and groups undergoing change pass through five separate stages: ignoring, attending, planning, executing and embedding. If we learn about these stages and understand how to recognize them, then we can take control of our organization's destiny and design a more effective, systematic change management plan.

It's worth noting that people rarely progress in a linear fashion from ignoring to embedding. In fact, they usually relapse to an earlier stage, sometimes several times. (Dieters know the truth of this observation. So do smokers, punsters and all those people who *really* are going to start exercising again next Monday, for sure.)

A second pattern that's worth noting is the appearance of change without the substance, where people conform to the change without being really committed to it (dieting all day and sneaking cake out of the freezer at night).

Stage One: Ignoring

At the *ignoring* stage, people have no intention of changing in the foreseeable future. They may be unaware of the need for change, or their awareness may be weak or incomplete; or they may be rejecting the knowledge. They may state that they wish to change, but this seems to be different from seriously intending to do so. Ignoring can be very stable, meaning that it is difficult to move out of; people may remain here for long periods of time.

Groups can also go through the ignoring stage; there's comfort in numbers. Groups do the same things as individuals, and people in groups may even seek support from each other for staying in the ignoring stage. They discuss facts and feelings related to the need for change, conclude that the need is weak or nonexistent and table the issue.

If some of the group, however, are in the next stage, *attending*, and have accepted the need for change, group interaction and discussion are more lively. Group members in the attending stage will try to win their ignoring colleagues over.

I'll give you an example. We see a lot of ignoring

whenever an organization introduces a new technology. Recently at a major consulting firm, the Meeting Maker software package was acquired, so that all of the consultants and their teams would know who would be where at any given time, and it would be easy to set up a meeting that all parties could attend. Many senior consultants resisted the use of this tool. They viewed it as an invasion of their privacy, a "Big Brother"-style lack of trust in their own planning and judgment. However, after about 75% of the firm was happily using the product, and showing up at meetings on time, the remaining "ignorers" quickly realized that the productivity benefits outweighed their concerns, and got onto the system.

Stage Two: Attending

People and groups in the *attending* stage are seriously intending to change in the future, but haven't yet made a clear commitment to act. (To return to our diet analogy, they buy 12 pounds of diet books and read them all, without actually adjusting any eating behaviors.) They seem not quite ready, and may put off acting for long periods. Because of this procrastination, the attending stage is also quite stable. People here are clearly aware of the need for change. They evaluate the pros and cons of the status quo as about equal. Groups discuss the likely benefits of change in detail and measure them against the time, effort and dollars needed to actually make the change.

This stage typically closes with a formal decision — to proceed or not. It is a critical point. Some members may not be ready to move to the next stage. How the group manages this, now and for the rest of the change, has an important bearing on success.

Here's an example. Working with a subsidiary of North American Life, I observed a group in the attending stage. The senior group wanted to implement a service quality program. Studies were commissioned. Meetings were held. Memos were drafted. But nothing was happening. Finally the leader asked the group what it would be worth to the business if the service quality program were implemented and worked. When responses ranged from $50,000 to $1 million, the group quickly realized that they needed to get beyond attending and put a realistic plan together with a demonstrable business case.

A Word about the First Two Stages

Ignoring suggests the existence of something to ignore: a real need for change. The question "Why change?" is central to ignoring, and to attending as well. Individuals and groups need a believable answer. That's why so much effort must go into building a case for change, identifying the pain, persuading colleagues who are still unaware of the need and justifying top-level decisions to other stakeholders — employees, customers, shareholders and so on.

A second question also requires time and effort: What

to change? People need to specify what needs to be changed, researching the status quo and the desired future state to clarify the content of the change. Identifying the "what?" successfully helps move the process out of these two early stages.

MANAGEMENT TIP:

Kickstarting your team out of the early stages

Here are three quick actions you can take as a senior executive to kickstart your team out of ignoring and/or attending:

1. Ask team members to build the case for change based on cost/benefit and productivity improvement.
2. Ask them what will happen if they don't make the change.
3. Restate your vision of the change and fire their imaginations — get some real enthusiasm flowing out of your dream.

Stage Three: Planning

At the *planning* stage, people intend to act in the very near future. They have thought carefully enough about taking action to actually develop a plan. The change at this stage is mostly in intent, although behavioral changes may also occur. This, then, is the first stage of external changes in behavior; in earlier stages only internal changes, in awareness and intent, occur.

Planning is not a very stable stage; people tend to progress relatively quickly to executing, or to fall into inertia. Countless task forces and legislative debates have come to nought because there was more pressure to create a plan than to create a difference. In these situations the momentum for change runs out once the initial hurdle — the creation of "the plan" — has been surmounted. The energy has gone into the planning of the change rather than into actually effecting change. (That's the stage where our dieter draws up an eating and exercise plan, committing words to paper, and posts it on the refrigerator.)

Conserve that energy. Groups at this stage are investing resources — time, energy, perhaps also dollars — in making plans for the action to come. Unlike the two previous stages, which likely involve all the members of the group, the activities of this stage may be carried out by one or a few members on behalf of the whole group.

Here's a planning example. A major North American financial services company was planning change and had set up a steering committee. This committee was cross-functional and looked at all staff functions to support the change. The committee put together a thorough change plan to advise the senior management team on what was required to make the change work. This team invested a serious level of time and energy in setting up the committee, reviewing processes and making recommendations.

Stage Four: Executing

In the *executing* stage, people change their actions or their environments significantly, at a major cost in time and energy. Changes here are the most visible and receive the most recognition. But equating executing with change is a mistake, because it overlooks the important internal cognitive and emotional work that prepares the way for action, as well as the work necessary to maintain the change later. Executing is the least stable of all the stages and has the highest risk of relapse. This is where the dieter spends money to join a health and fitness club. Signing up is a good sign — it's only a first step. The highest risk of relapse is at this stage.

Labatt Breweries is a good example. Leaders started making a major change in their business. They began to assign different activities to different resources — the staff, the executive team, outside consultants. And they also grouped work by function — there was a communications program, an education program, and a number of work-group teams and implementation teams assigned specific tasks. This company was executing change.

Stage 5: Embedding

People and groups at the *embedding* stage work to prevent relapse and consolidate their gains. Embedding is a period of continuing change, though most of it is internal rather than external. Ideas, attitudes and values shift gradually until they come to support the change. (Our dieter at this point actually prefers the taste of skim milk to whole milk and has lost the taste for rich desserts.) People continue to modify their actions or their environments to encourage the desired behavior and discourage relapse. This stage is more stable than Executing, but there is still substantial risk of relapse.

Groups try to stabilize the change at this point and make it habitual. This is real and necessary work; short-changing it may negate the gains achieved during the executing stage. Some of this work is obvious, like searching out and modifying any policies or procedures that run counter to the change. Some work is not so obvious, like the slow move of group norms and values into alignment with the change.

Sometimes embedding can encapsulate the entire change process very swiftly. A good friend of mine, a woman, was recently hired onto a previously all-male sales team. Their sales business mainly involved preparing and submitting major proposals to government departments. The woman had been used to using a personal computer at her previous company to prepare all of

Figure 3 — The Five Stages Of Change

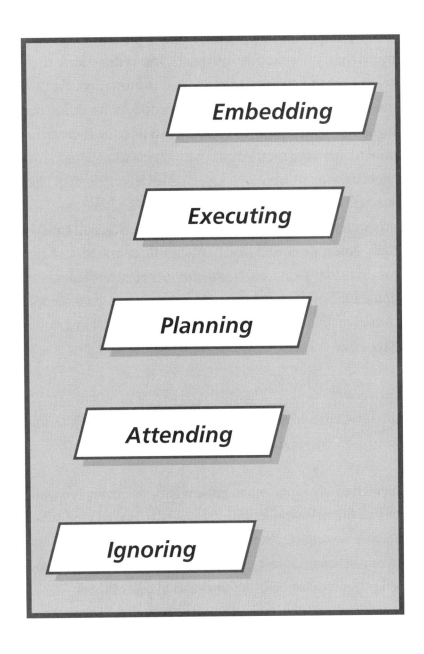

her own proposals, letters and memos. The culture of her new firm, however, was still oriented around a central word-processing support group, with the salesmen preparing information by hand for typing and then reviewing and correcting the typed information. At first the sales team ridiculed the woman openly for doing her own work: perhaps she would like to join the secretarial pool? The salesmen's time was much too valuable to spend keying in front of a screen! However, the men also soon observed two things: the woman was delivering five proposals for each of their own *and* she'd begun to lead their group in closed sales. Within three months of her joining the firm, each of the other four salesmen demanded and got his own PC. None now uses the pool.

From ignoring to embedding — it sometimes happens.

POP QUIZ:

What stage is your organization at?

If you have a change management initiative going forward, or you are planning it, you should try to understand what stage your organization has reached in the change process. Here are some characteristics of each stage; you should be able to recognize your organization in one of them.

1. *Ignoring:*
- People often ask: "Why should we change?"
- Managers write memos supporting the processes of the past.
- People are still doing their work the way they've always done it.

2. *Attending:*
- People show interest and ask questions, but then go back to old ways.
- There is no resource allocation to the change.
- There are verbal commitments, but no closure.

3. *Planning:*
- Time and money resources are allocated.
- A time schedule exists, with dates for achievements.
- All key stakeholders from all departments are involved.

4. *Executing:*
- The leaders of the organization are deeply involved.
- People's day-to-day activities are changing.
- Everyone is busier than usual, because most people are actually doing their old functions as well as their new activities.

5. *Embedding:*
- The new ways are part of everyday habits and processes.
- People wonder why anyone wouldn't do it this way.
- Your people become "missionaries" to other groups and organizations to try things this new way.

A Word about Relapsing

Have you ever seen someone work out a mathematical problem with a calculator, and then do it over in longhand because they still don't trust the machine? People are complex and carry the seeds of every change stage within them. The portrait we draw of the stages of change, with each following neatly on the heels of the other, oversimplifies what really happens. Real change is messy, fluid, dynamic, nonlinear. Nevertheless, the skeleton — successful change requiring progress through the five stages — remains.

"Relapse happens. The CEO may want change, and his senior team may smile and nod but not really be behind it; they may quietly try to subvert the process, even subconsciously, by always being 'too busy.' The leader must be vigilant and drag out the real concerns and objections; this takes a lot of time."

GEORGE FIERHELLER, VICE-CHAIRMAN, ROGERS COMMUNICATIONS

Part of the change dynamic is relapse. People rarely move directly from ignoring to embedding. In fact, in individual change, relapse is the rule rather than the exception. Ever tried to stay on a diet? How many times does a smoker quit before it finally works? The reality is that it may take two or three or more tentative moves to the executing or even to the embedding stage, with each followed by relapse, before success. The risk of relapse seems highest in the executing stage, next highest in the embedding stage. People don't invariably relapse to the first stage, ignoring, but they may move back to attending or planning. (Our dieter may fail to attend the health club but keep up the membership, and even join a support group to gain added motivation.)

It's as though participants learn what doesn't work from the failed attempts, then use this learning process to increase their chances of success later.

Relapses also occur in groups. As with individuals, they seem to happen in spite of the group's best efforts. Both individuals and groups may present relapses as deliberate decisions to abandon or postpone attempted change.

Relapsing is probably not as common in groups as it is in individuals, simply because of the peer influence of the group. It's less "acceptable" for a group to relapse than for an individual to do so. That's why support groups such as Weight Watchers help individuals achieve personal change more easily. There's a lesson there.

MANAGEMENT TIP:

Dealing effectively with a relapse

Here are some ideas and actions to bear in mind:

- Expect a relapse and prepare for it.
- Don't make your relapsed people (especially team leaders) feel like failures. Encourage them to try again, and keep trying.
- Pay immediate attention to the relapse. Don't be an "ignorer" yourself!
- If some groups have not relapsed, model others on their success.
- Involve everyone in making goals and commitments, and have everyone write them down. (A school superintendent who totally revolutionized public education in Modesto, California, nailed his eight new principles of education on the door of each school, for every teacher, student and parent to see.)

Why Change Fails

As change management consultants, working with organizations to help launch and accelerate change over the years, we have discovered a surprising problem. Many firms have great expectations; incisive strategic plans; bright minds at work; and an impressive level of activity. Yet the strategic implementation fails to live up to its advance billing; the hoped-for payoff is not realized. Change objectives seem to dissolve continually, leading to lost strategic vision, an expensive price-tag for unsatisfactory change, and higher blood pressure in the executive suite.

Industrial statistics support these observations of failure. An estimated 50% to 80% of mergers never live up to expectations. Less than 1% of medium and large U.S. companies have made acquisitions that improved their share price.

There is a very human answer to why strategies derail: they depend on *people* for successful execution, and massive change creates fear, confusion, and gaps in communication which cause people to draw back from the change.

The Fear of Change

We have all gone through change in our lives, both personally and professionally. On a grander scale, one might be excused for thinking that our species would be used to it. We have evolved from Neanderthal to Nintendo. We used to go outside to sniff the wind; now we look at satellite weather maps. Yet despite our collective history and experience of massive change, change still does not come easily to us. Each new change brings with it fresh fears that undermine our confidence: "Will I be successful? Will my security be threatened? Is this new thing what I want?"

"Most people prefer the status quo and see change
as a big dark unknown. You first have to get all
the key people to understand what you're trying to
achieve and what you need to do; why change
is necessary. Frank dialogue is critical; I am
constantly astounded at the thoughts people have
once you get them opening up. What you want are
disciples, not a passive audience."

DALE SISEL, PRESIDENT AND CEO (RETIRED)

RJ REYNOLDS TOBACCO INTERNATIONAL INC.

The fear of changing the status quo repeatedly sur-
faces during times of organizational change. When contemplating new strategies and significant organizational
shifts, leaders have an opportunity to ensure that their
organizations do in fact reach their strategic objectives,
instead of merely holding the false belief that they have.
Good human resource management may mean having
the right people in the right place at the right time, but it
also requires much more.

The Senior Management Chasm

Often the huge gulf between senior executives and
employees presents the greatest challenge to change. The
leader may clearly see the need to change while senior
executives "communicate" the new vision and mission,
tell people they are empowered and implore them to work

smarter, demonstrate leadership and be team players. On the other side of the gulf are middle managers and employees working in the trenches, trying to keep their heads above water and putting out fires. Middle managers struggle to understand what the change means for themselves and their people while employees question the need for change, cynically view change efforts as a new saddle on the old horse and complain that senior executives don't practice what they preach.

While the vision of change may be refreshing, the everyday commitments of the workforce do not disappear. The grass roots of the company still have to produce, and senior management must have an idea of what it means when — as far as employees are concerned — the earth is quaking beneath them. Marie Antoinette, when told there was not enough flour to allow the people of France to make bread (or enough bread), said, "Let them eat cake." If she had recommended eating apples instead she might have kept her head.

Lack of Context

Change often fails because employees understand neither the organizational system which they are a part of nor the connection between their behavior and the "big picture."

People often resist change because the mental models they hold about how their organization works are ingrained and implicit. These models are based on an outdated view of a market and economy that may no longer exist. More significantly, organizations are often unaware that employees have these models, or fail to appreciate the impact the models have on behavior. These assumptions help decide which information people choose to focus on, and the behaviors they choose to demonstrate.

A case in point is People Tech's work with Scott's Kentucky Fried Chicken. For decades this was a successful organization with high profits and a stable, loyal customer base. Within a short period revenues dropped dramatically, and so did profits. Yet many people within the organization did not see that these changes reflected a permanent erosion of their traditional customer base and changing consumer preferences, preferring instead to blame business results on the "bad economy." As one senior executive remarked prior to embarking on a major change initiative, "We still think we are a fat-cat organization living in the 1970s." Unless such outdated models are recognized and revised, organizational change efforts face a major uphill battle, and the gap between the organization's mental model and reality becomes ever wider.

MANAGEMENT TIP:

Ten ways to reduce resistance to change

1. Involve interested parties in the planning of change.
   - Ask them to provide you with data.
   - Ask them for suggestions: "How would your team work best?"
   - Incorporate their ideas.

2. Clearly define the need for the change.
   - Show how the strategic decision is being made.
   - Communicate the pain both personally and in written form. Put it "on the record."

3. Address the "people needs" of those involved. Disrupt only what needs to be changed. Help people retain friendships, comfortable settings and group norms wherever possible.

4. Have the group involved in planning the change announce the change.

5. Design flexibility into change.
   - Phase in change wherever possible, to allow people to complete current efforts and assimilate new behaviors.

- Allow workers to redefine their roles during the course of change.
- Be flexible as a leader — be prepared to change the change.
- Create a vent to ease the pressure of change. Hold open sessions that encourage the voicing of frustrations and then respond, "What can we do to help?"

6. Be open and honest.
   - Don't pretend that negative aspects of the change don't exist.
   - Don't try to maneuver employees or trick them, or keep secrets from them.
   - Be firm about making change, but allow workers to shape that change by showing them what they have the power to affect.

7. Do not leave openings for people to return to the status quo. If you and your organization are not ready to commit yourselves to the change, don't announce the strategy.

8. Focus continually on the positive aspects of the change. Be specific where you can: "30,000 jobs saved," "Faster distribution creates warehousing savings that can

be invested elsewhere," "Time spent writing
memos will be cut in half."

- Give workers a taste of things to come — use their
  suggestions, reward ideas, let them rewrite their
  job descriptions.

9. Look for areas of agreement between yourself and
people who oppose you.

- Humor can help you find common ground. Take a
  cue from Voltaire: "I disapprove of what you say,
  but I will defend to the death your right to say it."
- Show that you are working with your opponents
  to find a solution that addresses their concerns.
- Don't attack. It serves no useful purpose.

10. Look for training programs that deliver basic skills as
opposed to processes. I recommend programs on: con-
ducting meetings, team-building, self-esteem or gaining
control of your life, unleashing creativity, coaching.

- Include adequate retraining and adjustment
  mechanisms in plans for change.

Reinventing the Leader

Sensitive New Age management

·

Military models and the old-boy network

·

Leading versus managing

·

A 12-step program for old-style leaders

Are You the Right Person to Be Doing This?

Change is a Bill Clinton kind of job. So what happens if you're Richard Nixon?

Actually, something very interesting could result: the change you're making could change you. Here are some of the things I predict will happen to you if you undertake seriously the task of changing your corporation:

- You'll become a more interesting person. Your interests will be broader. You'll find yourself talking not just about what happened in your boardroom or your sales meeting, but about what's happening in other companies and other kinds of organizations. You'll read more widely and more deeply.

- People will like to talk to you more. That's not just because you'll know more interesting things, but because you'll have learned that listening is a primary ingredient in learning from a conversation. It'll strike you early in the process that nobody learns much with their mouth open.

- You'll become a more effective executive. People will be more likely to act on what you say, because they'll have learned that your decisions are founded on a variety of sources: you've listened before you've spoken. You'll be a more effective leader because you'll have a vision that you can articulate passionately — and that people can buy into willingly.

- You'll have more fun; tons more. And you'll find that fun is powerfully productive. Fun doesn't necessarily mean giggles. Fun can be the kind of satisfaction you get from a trout dinner when you've caught the trout yourself.

Change is a big step that requires courage and risk. It demands an emotional commitment from the executive team and/or the board. An emotional commitment is something more than "Yo, boss" or "I think I see the millennium, chief, and I *like* it." An emotional commitment always has sweat stains on it.

> "Definition of a mid-life crisis: when the skills that helped you survive the first half of your life are killing you in the second half."
>
> WENDY BURNS, PSYCHOTHERAPIST

We have to remember, however, that change can occur very slowly, year after year. It can take place so slowly that we lose the overall vision, get caught up in daily frustrations and fall prey to "short-termism."

Because of all this, it's essential for the leader to create and follow vision-driven strategy. Bill Gates may not know where his recent shift of Microsoft to an ideal of total connectivity will lead the company, but his absolute commitment to that vision will keep them on that course until they arrive.

When interviewing CEOs in preparing this book, we were surprised at how often they remarked that they had never realized that, in making changes to their organizations, they would have to change so much about themselves. This makes sense. Most of those who are leaders today were trained to be leaders in the old style. The autocratic management learned only too well. But that doesn't mean that it was their natural tendency, or that they can't change. But it takes a lot of work to make the change. It also takes great pain, and any leaders who aren't experiencing pain should be suspicious of their own process. If you're having no pain, you're not growing. You are engaged in maintaining your present stature.

If this sounds like touchy-feely, sensitive New Age management, it isn't. It requires strength and endurance to channel your energy in new ways.

> "Training is necessary, but hardly sufficient in helping employees with organizational change. Communicating goals is essential; people like to feel connected to the values of the enterprise, to see where they fit in. Disconnection is a source of organizational stress."
>
> SHEILA WELLINGTON, CEO, CATALYST

Coaching is a topic that's been talked about for years. But many of us have talked about it in "Rah, rah ... keep it up, team!" terms. That's nice and necessary — but it's not the type of coaching I want you to think about.

It's time for coaching by:

1) thinking,
2) designing,
3) showing,
4) demonstrating.

In fact, "coaching" may be too abstract a word. What we may need today are quarterbacks instead of coaches:

people who are actually playing on the field. Players who are adding value themselves, rather than standing on the sidelines telling others what to do.

Think about it. When you first went down a ski hill, you fell — everybody does. The fall caused pain — physical and mental. That pain motivated learning. You don't get that pain as a coach; you get it from actually playing the sport. You don't learn to avoid the pain through cheerleading; you learn through experience. And you learn best and fastest from someone who's out there with you.

> "It is possible to effect change even in the most traditional, conservative areas. Abitibi-Price is a large, old and historic firm in the very traditional forest products industry. Yet today the executive team all, quite unselfconsciously, refer to themselves as "coaches" and "the coaching team." This is now how they see themselves. They actually changed the labels first, and the thinking followed."
>
> ANNE FAWCETT, MANAGING PARTNER,
> THE CALDWELL PARTNERS INTERNATIONAL

In the old days, CEOs surrounded themselves with staff. They formed a kind of protective unit, their own little Secret Service. One CEO, the head of a major high-tech manufacturing firm, literally surrounded himself with a phalanx of staff, almost as if they were bodyguards.

What were they for? They were to ensure that he had all the information at his fingertips. They were to ensure that he had all the answers; that everything was prepared, and there would be no sense of failure. They were there to ensure there was a distance between him and the rest of the world. The distance was somehow equated with respect: the greater the distance, the greater the leader. God was in his heaven, Nixon was closeted in the White House, and the corporate maximum leader was beyond shoulder-rubbing distance. From this lofty vantage point, the Maximum Leader seldom ventured down to the mire below. He (it was usually a he) didn't see the actual people doing the actual work — or the consumers doing the actual consuming — he saw beautifully-crafted organizational and distribution charts.

Unfortunately though the charts showed — usually in four colors — *where* the people were, they didn't show why or the fact that they were communicating with each other using lines that weren't on the chart at all. In fact, the lines were melting. But from the Presidential Suite and over the shoulders of the Presidential Guard, the leader couldn't see it happening.

Some of that — incredibly — is still happening. Leaders are still confusing writing memos about empowerment and issuing newsletters about two-way communication with actually getting out and doing it. They have no personal contact with the shop floor. They don't talk regularly to anyone actually out selling to the ultimate customer. They have no real intimacy with their corporation. The leader knows all the tidy facts and figures, but doesn't know the messy truth.

Leaders have trouble with the word "intimacy": they think it's something that only comes out of the mouths of afternoon talk show hosts or Alan Alda. But think it over: Napoleon made a point of hanging out with the troops. So did George Patton. Neither called it "intimacy" but that's what it was. And that intimacy gave them a real view of what actually happened that commanders who confined themselves to the view from the hilltop didn't have. They knew whether the troops were being fed, whether the bullets fit the rifles, whether the newly issued boots were rotting off the marchers' feet. "Intimacy" wasn't a wuss word: it's what you had to have to win.

Both the leaders mentioned also had a real sense of clarity: a clear vision of what they desired. In both cases the vision was a little frightening, but it did let them focus on exactly where they were going — which made getting there a lot easier. The kind of clarity I'm talking about involves more than wanting to achieve all the items highlighted in next year's strategic plan. It involves a vision — which is another word leaders have a bunch of trouble with. They think it's a "soft" word, the kind of word they'd throw around during a board meeting of a L.A. herbal tea company. Let's clear that up: I'll give you a few "visions," and you tell me the executive who had them, whether the vision is working and whether the leader is flaky or not:

- "I want anyone to be able to send a parcel across the country — door-to-door — in a day."
- "I want to design a computer anyone can use."
- "I want to start a 24-hour television news channel anyone can tune into."
- "I want to build a compact car in the USA that will be worth more and cost less than Japanese competition."

What usually stands between a leader and a vision is a wall of paper, the clamor of memos, the roar of meetings, the jangle of phones. You can't have a vision with all that stuff going on.

We use a process for leaders that — ahem — actually has them look at themselves. In case you have the same problem with "self-examination" that you had with "vision" and "clarity," I'm going to explain the concept in military terms. More macho, you know. And if it reassures you any further, my Harley can beat your Harley.

The Military Model

The best military leadership comes from personal example. The best commander eats the same food as his men *after* they have eaten. At some point in the commander's career, rifles were cleaned, boots were polished, latrines were dug, sergeants were obeyed. Stop for a moment and contrast that with the work experience of MBAs who have seldom shared the experience of the people who work under them. They become lieutenants without having fired a gun and very few of them take the time to find out how it's done after they join the organization.

That's nice and clean and tidy. But it *does* make things like "intimacy" difficult. And it also makes having a successful vision almost impossible. After all, you can't have a successful vision unless you can share it. And sharing it is tough unless you really know the troops and what they're doing. If you doubt this, read a slim volume called *Rivethead* by Ben Hamper. Written by a veteran of a GM line, it shows what happens to a corporate vision like "quality" when the leader doesn't actually know what's happening in the trenches — and when the people in the trenches don't know why management is sending around a person disguised as a cat to talk to them about "quality." It's a devastating view of "rule by memo" and "leadership by sloganeering" as opposed to leading by example.

Your management must understand the people working for them. And the people working for them must understand the vision of management. In the Gulf War, the first objective of the alliance was to destroy Iraq's command and control structure. With the head cut off, the body died. There was no understanding of the strategic objectives by the forces in the field. In successful military organizations, that wouldn't have happened: the person pulling the trigger would have known — and agreed with — the broad strategy. That person would also know — and agree with — the near-term tactics. They could go on without hourly orders. They could improvise and improve on their tactics. They aren't tin soldiers being moved around a carpet by military theorists: they are people with an immediate view of the real situation who are empowered to take action. They can achieve their leaders' military vision better and faster.

Winston Churchill had been a prisoner of war. He'd been fired on and had fired back. He was only prevented from being in a boat during D Day by the personal intercession of the King. During the war he kept a gun by his side and was an expert with it. He talked to his people in the most personal way possible. Pick a favorite military leader. Read the biography. You'll find that in almost every case the leader knew how to dig a trench and still maintained contact with the people in the trenches when he no longer had to.

Do you and your management do anything like that? Really? If so, send me the name of your company and its NYSE symbol.

The Historical Parallels of Thought and Leadership

Psychological theory holds that there are three kinds of intelligence: verbal (inductive) reasoning; numeric reasoning (linear, deductive); and symbolic reasoning, the ability to put unlike things together and use metaphor and simile (this is the type of reasoning behind the "chaos theory").

In the 1950s and 1960s, corporate leaders were often drawn from marketing (verbal reasoning). In global politics, there was a parellel trend: the great "marketers" included JFK, Lester Pearson and Fidel Castro. In the 1960s and 1970s, the typical corporate leader was a number-cruncher, an analytical type (numeric reasoning). In politics we saw the cool pragmatists: Lyndon Johnson, Edward Heath, Pierre Trudeau, François Mitterrand. Starting in the 1980s and especially now in the 1990s, the ideal leader is often plucked from an entirely different industry to bring a new way of thinking to the table (symbolic reasoning: Pepsi's CEO moves to Apple, Campbell Soup's CEO moves to publishing). On the political scene we see the rise of "poet as president" (Vaclav Havel); President Bill Clinton plays saxophone. Leaders are required to be more well-rounded human beings. Entrepreneurs do particularly well in this category.

Too many leaders in the past were driven by their own insecurity. In a recent issue of *Fortune* magazine, a partner at the McKinsey Corporation was quoted as saying that the firm looks to hire people who are "very smart, insecure and thus driven by their insecurity, and competitive." That is a negative way to lead: to be the top, to be the best, to have to prove to yourself that you are good enough (although this has not been my experience with the McKinsey partners I know personally). Leaders do not need to prove that they are good enough. Yes, they have wisdom, experience, knowledge, ideas. But primarily, they know how to be facilitators, to bring people's expertise together to ensure that organizations survive. They believe in themselves and, most important, they believe in others.

Leading versus Managing

We must also remember, as Abraham Zaleznik reminds us in an article in the *Harvard Business Review*, that there is a difference between leaders and managers. Even in today's flattened corporate structures, the process of management will still be required. That involves delegation, accountability, structure and systems. Leaders are navigators. They map the route that will help their organizations keep pace with global change. The faster the car is going, the clearer the map has to be and the more familiar the leader must be with various shortcuts, potholes, rest stations, etc. That's why this book is aimed at leaders. And leaders are everywhere in the organization, not just at the top.

The Benefits of Reinventing the Leader

What can changing leadership style mean to an organization and its employees?

- an environment that people feel good about, supported in, and enjoy working in;
- people who want the company to succeed, who care enough to put out extra effort;
- loyalty;
- willingness to accept some of the difficulties we face today: less real income, fewer perks, having to meet greater expectations with fewer resources;
- role modeling. Leadership is not the sole responsibility of the CEO, but most organizations take their cue from the top. Strong leadership leads to the demonstration of leadership by the rest of the management team.

Changing Your Mind

We said that, to change your organization, you first have to change yourself. How do you do it? How do you make personal changes? As in all progress, you take it one step at a time. Here are some steps that leaders as individuals can take:

- Know your own mind. Make a list of your most basic assumptions about yourself and the way the world works. For example: "I believe that hard work brings rewards. I believe democracy is the best method of government." Go over your list and ask yourself where these beliefs come from.

- Widen your perspectives by paying attention to fleeting thoughts. Keep a "Today I learned" line in your daily scheduler and actively mine for insights. Here's one week of perspectives, to give you an idea:

Today I learned/today I noticed that:
- *My secretary is scared of me. I realized I didn't know when her birthday is or what she likes to eat for lunch.*
- *My kids have more fun playing pretend than playing with toys. I realized that nifty technology is no guarantee that a need will be fulfilled.*
- *There is no good place to sit outside in the heart of Toronto's financial district. I wondered if this was done deliberately to discourage loitering. I realized I don't go outside enough.*
- *The supermarket sells some spatulas next to the pancake mix. I realized how many buying decisions are based on convenience and the power of suggestion.*

> *— My suit was incredibly uncomfortable. I realized I'm a victim of fashion and traditional corporate expectations.*

Once you have these insights on paper, you can study their implications and apply your findings. Insight leads to more insight, and is the basis for sophistication.

- Put into place a continuous upward-feedback system that ensures you receive feedback from your people on your own strengths and weaknesses at least every six months. Be open: are you particularly frightened of someone in the mail room? Is he or she frightened of you?

POP QUIZ:

Rest in Peace

In order to enhance your understanding of yourself and others, try this compelling exercise: write your own epitaph. Actually, write two: the one you would like to see written; and the one others might write if you died today.

With more perspective you will be able to re-examine your leadership and its priorities.

Consider:

- *Time commitments.* Most of the CEOs inter-
viewed for this book spent 50% to 80% of their
time managing their organization's change.
- *Behavior.* If all you do is react to situations, you must
learn to let this go. Stop racing around putting out
fires. Make sure you're lighting a few of your own.
- *Communications style.* Most CEOs believe they
are excellent communicators, but their public and
employees know better. How many and what kind
of people do you talk to on a daily basis?
- *Tools for aligning people with strategy.* Skills of
participation and delegation will become critical;
you must learn how to bring people along with you.
- *Education.* More than ever, you must attend to
your own professional development.
- *Vulnerability.* The leaders of the future will share
concerns and feelings with their team.
- *Self-esteem.* The fact is that many top leaders
were driven to overachieve out of a fundamental
sense of inferiority. Even if it means getting professional counseling, the leaders of the future will
need a healthy love of self.

What Kind of Leader Are You?

Changes in your mind should lead to adjustments in your
style. Insight and perspective will reveal that how you

make decisions and guide your workforce is at least as important as the decisions themselves. The quality of your decisions depends on your ability to achieve a holistic view of your company's workings and their greater contexts. Tailor your style to eliminate your blind spots.

> "The CEO must live his values — coming in early, attending meetings, imparting a sense of urgency and purpose. You can't lay down the law without doing it yourself; you have to lead by example. People will test you; miss a deadline on purpose to test the CEO. "
>
> MAX STREBEL, PRESIDENT AND CEO, UNION BANK OF SWITZERLAND

Begin by knowing what kind of leader you are now. Use this definition by *Source*.

- *Transactional leaders* hold few personal values. They are involved in a pure trade-off between contractees: you do this and I'll do this and we'll both win. This style will effect change, but without loyalty or passion.

- *Charismatic leaders* are focused only on their own visions. For success they must get others to subscribe to their visions. This calls for devotion and a willing sacrifice by the followers. If the leaders are successful in this, however, the changes can be powerful ones (this is the model for most major Western religions).

- *Transformational leaders* do transact, but are holding out an honest vision which appeals to higher virtues in the follower. The follower is able to buy into the leader's vision with no sacrifice of personal values. This style gains the greatest commitment.

An Action List for Building Leadership and Loyalty

- *Be the example.* In one consulting firm I know of, the president was the first in the organization to move into a small cubicle when space and restructuring demanded it. Later, he also became the first employee to share a cubicle.

- *Trim away the perks.* If you still have an executive parking spot, executive dining room and executive washroom, re-examine whether those privileges add value to your work or whether they just take away from the self-esteem of others.

- *Engage in Management by Walking Around (MBWA).* In the military, MBWA involves getting out and talking to the men. A MBWA pioneer was Malcolm Gittings at Hewlett-Packard Canada (at time.) Each day he would enter the building from a different door, so that in heading to his office he moved past different people each day, and chatted with them briefly and casually. This proved more effective than the sometimes contrived presidential walkabout, which imparts about as much useful information as a receiving line at a wedding.

- *Be a real person.* Show vulnerability. Nothing is more moving in a leader than taking the mask off and demonstrating deeply held emotions. This can be uncomfortable for leaders raised in a more traditional environment, but once you take the leap, you will feel more connected to other people.

- *Understand yourself and your motivations.* People now expect this of you. Put yourself through a feed-back assessment process; understand what it is you need to look at and what the key things are that you need to do in the future.

- *Know your bottom line.* It's important to distinguish between those business activities and essentials that can be done by others, and those things that only you can or must do — allocate capital, for example.

- *Foster relationships outside the internal organization* — with suppliers, customers and even competitors. In the new "webbed" organization (see Chapter 10), there is no fixed boundary. This is strikingly different from the old model in which leaders and employees of rival firms would leave a room to avoid speaking.

- *Understand that you carry you with you* wherever you go. Sound too Zen? All this means is that our personal relationships do affect our business, whether our predecessors recognized this or not. Whom you meet changes your business. Great leaders absorb from everyone, and even get fantastic new ideas from a chat with a seatmate on a plane.

- *Use your free time to make trouble.* That is, make your free time just that: task-free. Use it to create, think laterally, play. Deliberately build creative free time into your lifestyle and your business will be richer for it.

- *Make sure you're always having fun and you're always doing business.* Since, in the new organization, everything connects, beware of attempting to box life into family, work and vacation blocks — it just doesn't work. You can't force "fun" and "quality time." Sound like a recipe for burnout or workaholism? Not at all, if you're always having fun in your work.

• *Always be curious* — a precondition for learning. Leaders get involved in matchmaking, even if it doesn't put money in their pockets in the first instance. Leaders love to spot and create or optimize opportunities. They are collectors of people, networkers without immediate self-interest. This new leadership has also created a new era in recruiting; increasingly, you meet or spot someone whom you instinctively know you want in your organization. So you create a job for that person, one which would not have existed without that unique individual. The new leader engages in *use* without *abuse*. There is a social contract: I deliver and add value to you, you will be valuable to me. A long-term relationship of mutual benefit is created.

• *Have passion.* Passion is infectious.

• *Replenish.* Leaders must learn the art of introspection. Only looking within will bring true relief from pain, whether the replenishment takes the form of meditation or physical activity. Leaders must break out of the logic-box, the grind, the gerbil-wheel of activity that has kept so many of them thinking in a linear fashion.

A Twelve-Step Program for
Old-Style Leaders

1. Admit that it's time to find a style for the 1990s.
2. Believe that you can change your ways.
3. Make a new social contract.
4. Make a fearless inventory of your short-comings.
5. Share your findings with others in the organization.
6. Learn new skills in team-building and interpersonal relations.
7. Align your organizational systems to support the new order.
8. Recognize the extended family of your customers, suppliers, etc.
9. Empower your stakeholders.
10. Check back from time to time to take stock and make adjustments.
11. Work on your own self-esteem.
12. Influence your industry peers to adopt the new style.

How Do I Get Everybody Else On This Boat?

CHAPTER SEVEN

Cultural Antibodies in the Organization

Last year's five-year plan

·

Corporate antibodies

·

The cult of the "policies and procedures" manual

·

Alignment

·

Sacred cows

"The old command-and-control behavior is finished. We used to have rules for when things went wrong; now, our motto is 'do away with a rule a month.'"

PETER MAURICE, VICE-CHAIR, CANADA TRUST FINANCIAL SERVICES

STUCK IN A HOTEL room on the road, I sometimes succumb to afternoon television. It's healthier than the tequila in the mini-bar, but just as good at numbing the mind. Two or three hours of it and I'm probably unfit to operate heavy equipment.

What strike me are the commercials. If all you knew about North America was what you knew from the commercials on afternoon television, you'd conclude it was populated by a race that was almost permanently ravaged by flu symptoms, grossly overweight and in constant need of communicating with psychics over the phone.

We have parallel malaises on the corporate level. Managers are worried by strange symptoms. We're going through terminal angst about rightsizing. And we're always calling consultants.

This is human behavior; we're a jittery species. We're always reaching out for new cures and new hopes. And just as consistently we resist what they offer. The rowing machine goes into the closet. The pills pile up in the medicine cabinet. We switch from psychic to astrologer hoping someone else has a new, improved future for us.

Doing a check of studies at an international packaged-goods company, I came across a strange and very enlightening document. It was insightful, incisive and in tune with the company's customer base. I asked the person who was helping me what it was. "That," he said, "is *last* year's five-year plan."

I think part of the problem is that we're so eager for improvement and change that we never quite get around to making it. It's more fun to have furniture catalogues than a living room. It's more engaging to listen to management consultants than to manage.

Organizational Systems That Hold You Back

Antibodies are great in the human body. They fight germs.

They battle foreign organisms. They keep us healthy.

Where we don't have the natural antibodies, science has worked to deliver them. That's why we get vaccinated. Edward Jenner, an English scientist came up with the idea. He was appalled at the spread of smallpox in his country. He wondered why the human body couldn't fight it. And he came up with the idea that if the human body learned to fight a weaker version of the disease, it could ultimately defeat the disease itself.

He found a weaker version of the disease in cows: cowpox. ("Vaccination" gets its name from the Latin for "cow.") He injected blood from a cow suffering from cowpox into humans and found that humans who were injected could resist smallpox.

But while antibodies help us fight off harmful invaders, they also reject foreign bodies that are essential to our survival-like transplanted organs.

Organizations have antibodies too — and those antibodies wage powerful (and often successful) war against new ideas.

There are companies with vast three-ring binders full of antibodies; they're called "policies and procedures" manuals and they're just chock full of dicta that impede the companies' ability to change.

But policies and procedures are far from being the only obstacles to change in your organization. Here are other major ones:

- computer architecture which supports old ways of working;
- recruiting methods that hire the same kind of people over and over again;
- work spaces designed to divide workers rather than bring them together;
- performance evaluations or other human resource systems locked into old ways of *behaving;*
- formal and informal company traditions;
- organization charts that fail to change with the times;
- the skill sets of the workforce ("I wasn't trained for that");
- standards based on old corporate expectations rather than on real "quality" requirements.

Let's take compensation or incentive systems, for example. There is a move away from individual work toward teamwork, as organizations become complex and no one individual holds the answer. Most of our compensation systems have been based on individual rewards rather than team rewards. Leaders have been afraid to move toward team rewards because they feared diluting accountability. *For the compensation system to work, it must reward the team, if the team is the unit that is required to get the work done.* That doesn't mean there can't be a component of the compensation that applies to individual accountability. There has been much work done in the compensation area with regard to the rewarding of the acknowledged worker and the reinforcement of team behavior.

The point is that you can't get out of the status quo if you don't compensate differently, because no matter what you tell people you want from them, your rewards contradict your message.

Try this: go through the contents of your in-basket, E-mail and voice-mail and make a list of the sources of the materials contained in it. Note the method of delivery beside each source. Note how many people it took to bring the material to you (i.e. how many names are at the bottom of a report?). Now note the dates associated with the materials. Study the list, looking for its bureaucratic implications. You should end up with a fairly clear (though admittedly unscientific) picture of where the red tape — unnecessary procedures and systems — lies in your company.

Now get out your scissors and get ready to cut.

When in Doubt, Throw It Out

If your workers can't tell you why a given piece of paper requires three signatures before it can be sent on, chances are it doesn't need them. If they can't explain the need for printing out three copies of something available on the computer, then, three copies likely aren't needed. Red tape accumulates like leftovers at the back of the fridge, and should be approached with the same ruthless practicality: get rid of anything that's moldy or unappetizing or has been sitting on the bottom shelf since you moved in.

Pick a day, any day, and have everyone in the company make a list of what he or she does and why (e.g. "Called accounting to get approval on revised budget; setup a meeting for Thursday to go over first draft of new telemarketing plan."). To ensure honesty, ask that the lists be anonymous. Have each worker rate the importance of each activity, according to its perceived ultimate value to the bottom line, on a scale of 1 to 5. Now have your team managers consolidate the lists of their workers and offer *their* perceived value ratings. Your managers should look at ways of eliminating activities that everyone agrees are of low value.

Alignment is the key to evaluating your systems. The systems, procedures and beliefs of the entire organization must align with the strategic intent of the leaders. Once the systems have been changed, however, it is important that people understand them — understand their intent, understand they're not perfect and understand how to use them.

Performance Management System

System for setting individual goals for employees and measuring those goals against the performance of an individual at the end of an annual cycle.

Let's look at the performance management system.

This system is the most essential tool for reinforcing behavior, and it's probably the system that most organizations would say has failed. Part of the problem is likely that the system design is not in line with the strategy. In fact, often the human resource departments that design the performance management systems are not privy to the strategy (at least, that has been true in the past), so performance is rated independently from its contribution to strategy. Aligning performance with strategy is absolutely critical if we're going to create a webbed organization — which is our goal, as you will see in Chapter 10.

The lesson is that if you don't tell everyone what's happening — or devise a way for change to *really* happen — nothing is going to happen. And nothing is going to happen for a long, long time before you hear about it.

Breaking Down the Antibodies

When Arthur Young (predecessor to Ernst & Young) was going through its change process, the firm supported interrelated consulting engagements in which strategy, compensation and performance management areas were examined both separately and together. The firm reasoned that, if it was going to ask its people to do new things, then the organization should change the ways in which it rewarded and evaluated them. The project involved all of the senior partners of the firm.

Be prepared for resistance from some workers.

Remember how important the performance management system may be to them. They have to understand how changes will benefit them, so that they won't feel threatened by your efforts at "cutting the fat." They can't be afraid of restructuring themselves out of a job.

Try these rewards for high-quality suggestions from your teams:

- Give away "training points" — a certain number of points earns opportunities for education and skills updating, paid for by the company and chosen by the recipients (to be taken at times of their choosing and at the institutions of their choice).
- Give them what they want. The quality of the suggestion dictates the dollar level of your generosity.
- Offer them part of the dividend. If an idea saves the company money, give them a percentage of that.

Running Compatibility Checks

Management information systems are another prime problem area. Let's say that a new application is created to collect key inventory data from each store in a large hardware chain. Only certain people can access this critical data, or input to it. In the meantime, the same company initiates an empowerment program allowing line people to do inventory; however, this behavior is not consistent with the new system. Then the organization wonders why its empowerment program hasn't worked out. The bottom line is that systems must be built to be compatible with the overall strategy, and new strategies can't be implemented unless all systems have been re-examined for compliance — in an impact analysis.

Let's take a look at the whole picture by focusing on a case study. We'll look at one company and what it had to do to make its new vision work. The Campbell Soup Company is one of North America's largest and most successful food processing organizations, most famous for its canned condensed soup.

Case Study: Campbell Soup

In 1992 Campbell's CEO, John Cassaday, initiated a major change process that began with a sweeping, new vision. It was expressed as *"Fastest gate to plate,"* and called for a strategy of striving for absolute freshness in taste, while maintaining the lowest possible cost to the consumer. The strategy implied making significant changes to Campbell Soup's methods of distribution, its relationships with farmers and suppliers and its approaches to refrigeration and storage.

In moving toward *"Fastest gate to plate,"* Campbell faced major challenges, particularly amongst its systems. It had created, over the decades of its existence, a large bureaucracy, and old ways of thinking and working were entrenched in a tenured workforce.

To overcome these challenges, Campbell needed to alter both its belief systems and its support systems. Its organizational beliefs now had to encompass:

- nimbleness,
- short runs,
- quicker decisions,
- empowerment of workers,
- TQM (total quality management) at the line level, and
- supplier empowerment.

When we looked at the company's systems, we saw that it was necessary to alter each one so that it supported the new strategy. Performance management systems needed to encourage fast turnover, not just volume sales at the end of the year. In recruiting, high initiative became valued. Compensation plans rewarded partnerships, and encouraged buyers not just to get the best price from a supplier, but to strive for higher quality of ingredients. Training and development programs helped employees to understand their client, the consumer. The management information system no longer merely tracked production volume, costs and sales, but helped users focus on quality, response time and gathering customer feedback. The company's communications style also became more customer-focused; more collaborative than competitive.

Inhumane Resources

Many business executives think of their organizational systems as things, not people: distribution, manufacturing, supply. However, for true "system" solutions, the people element must be addressed. For example, as you read this chapter you may be thinking that you need to solve a problem in your management information system or your production system. Instead, your solutions should have labels like these:

* urgency and pace;
* ownership;
* trust;
* collaboration;
* new ways of contracting;
* shared measures;
* new skills — TQM, customer focus, relationship building.

Your human resources team should be structured to coordinate team efforts to work together, facilitate team networking and support the teams' training and incentive needs. Too many Human Resource departments are designed to keep track of "who is where on the corporate ladder." Kick the ladder down and you'll help put your workers on the level.

MANAGEMENT TIP:

Homework

How well do you know your company, really? Have you actually read your own policies and procedures manual cover to cover? Do you know exactly what is going on in human resources? What kind of job descriptions do people have and are they accurate? What image do you project to suppliers, competitors?

Before you start changing your company, you're going to need a view of it from the bottom up. Start by pretending you are a junior clerk applying for a job and doing research on the company. Gather up all the printed information you can get your hands on (that includes things like application forms and the stuff that gets put on the bulletin boards) and spend a weekend trying to get a newcomer's impression of the organization. Read between the lines; if you had no other source of information, how would your company strike you? Traditional? Progressive? Innovative? Conservative? A people place? A by-the-book place? Would the company hire you because of your credentials or because of your accomplishments?

Now try to compare what you've read with how things really work. For example, if you were a junior clerk with a bright idea, where would you take it? Who would listen? Has the company ever acted on a junior's ideas? Why not?

A Word About Sacred Beasties

The temples of our corporations shelter whole herds of "sacred cows" — or traditions and beliefs that are never questioned because they are — well, they just *are*. Leaders implementing a dynamic change vision can be foiled by these seemingly harmless beasts. They have to go.

Once, we worked with the North American division of a major Japanese car company. Except for the CEO and the vice-president of finance, who were Japanese, all of the senior management team were North American; middle management was split between Japanese and North American. Their sacred cow was that they needed, for the sake of their own ideas about teamwork, to pretend that there were no cultural differences between Japanese and North American people. Problems that were arising out of perfectly natural cultural differences could never be aired and resolved. When much remains unspoken, we tend to attribute sinister motives to behaviors that may be entirely innocent. For example, the Japanese team members liked to lunch together once a week, speaking Japanese. Their motivation was simple homesickness; they enjoyed being able to relax together and talk about things that interested them. But the North Americans felt not only excluded but suspicious: Were they being talked about? Were plots being hatched? Both sides often felt frustrated by the different business approaches of the other: the Japanese put a priority on consensus-building, no matter how long the process took; the North Americans tended to make decisions more swiftly than the Japanese liked.

Why couldn't they talk about being different? Well, they just couldn't — they thought it wasn't "right" somehow. Why not? Those differences could have been useful to them in the course of their business. And in avoiding a dialogue about their differences the teams managed to alienate each other.

To get these people to work their problems through, we needed to encourage them to break their taboo and acknowledge their differences. This was accomplished partly through a role-playing session in which the two camps engaged in role reversal. The Japanese managers had to pretend they were North Americans, and describe their Japanese colleagues (themselves) to the group. Interestingly, each group was much harder on its members than their colleagues would have been, revealing their own insecurities and fears in the process. Eventually, by getting all of the issues out into the open and by acknowledging that it was okay to ascribe some behaviors to cultural differences, the team was able to work together much more happily.

One of the most insidious sacred cows is "business planning." Planning processes should be aligned with change and quality initiatives, but often aren't. The organization and its planning systems tend to run on parallel tracks which never meet. The only thing worse, in terms of effective change management, than the old mistake of *"ready, fire, aim"* is the often-seen "aim, aim, aim!" in which nothing, it seems, is ever actually done. Business planning offers the seductive illusion of control, without delivering change.

MANAGEMENT TIP:

Recognizing sacred cows

Other sacred cows take the form of often-heard and rarely challenged comments made around the management table. You should listen for these telltale statements:

- "Never take on anything new."
- "Don't stop doing this, just add this."
- "It's always worked for us in the past."
- "Is this really required?"
- "I've seen this before and it won't work."
- "This system works ok now."
- "We have a system that would cost too much to redesign."
- "They said that last year and nothing happened."
- "They say that for the public but they don't mean it."

Aligning people, systems and strategies can be incredibly powerful. We can understand this more easily by taking a new look at an old case history. Years ago, American Airlines set a precedent for the strategic use of information systems by building SABRE, an online reservation system which was made available to travel agents. This system gave American Airlines the dominant market share for years afterward. For decades now, this case has been written about and held up as the ultimate justification for increased investment in computer systems, because analysts have generally assumed that the business success was a direct result of the implementation of the online computer system. Recently, however, some observers have suggested that perhaps American Airlines' success should also be attributed to their people: their service excellence, commitment to the customer and so on, which worked along with the management information system to create added value. American Airlines had (knowingly or otherwise) aligned their people and their systems with their strategy to be a world-leading airline. That is why the change worked.

CHAPTER EIGHT

The Terrifying Power of the Group

Groups and hunting parties

·

Good guys, bad groups and others

·

Group-to-group communications

It's Better in Groups

My insurance agent has two secretaries. For years the two have sat at two desks facing each other.

Being human, they chat. About who's being traded from the Jays. About the best place to buy low profile tires. About politics.

Being human, my insurance agent one day decided that the chat was counterproductive. That both secretaries would be more efficient if they had privacy from each other. That, in short, "they'd get more work done if they stopped the blathering." A wall was put up between the two secretaries.

Three weeks later the wall was taken down.

Turns out that while they were talking baseball, tires and politics, they were also talking business. "The quote on Mrs. Ogden's fender is $309," "Mr. Wallingford is two days late with his check again," "We need a new case of double density diskettes."

With the wall up, information was halved. If one secretary was out of the office, the access to facts dropped 50%. And, my insurance agent noted, productivity dropped because instant access to facts was blocked by . . . a wall.

Two people. That's the smallest group possible. But a group of two, my insurance agent found, can do the work of a group of 2.5.

Imagine what a group of seven can accomplish.

The First Group

Most of us got our first taste of "group dynamics" at the dinner table each night. We soon discovered, through instruction, observation and osmosis, what was and was not acceptable behavior. As children we came to understand what was okay to talk about: our day, our accomplishments, playful anecdotes. We also learned what was not okay: anger, conflict, negative expressions. An enormous amount of learning, in fact, takes place in our first group experience.

Our next group experiences occur when we begin to move out into the world as children: into school and other social or community settings. Once again we learn sets of explicit and implicit rules about how to operate as part of a team or group. We are sometimes given conflicting instructions: we must share our toys, paints and books with the others, but we are also competing with the others for grades and the teacher's attention. As team members, we become highly competitive against other teams. This, by the way, is a phenomenon not found in all cultures. We begin inevitably to form our own approaches to group membership.

Each of us takes those attitudes and behaviors we learned with us into the workplace. We encounter others whose first group experiences may have been entirely different from ours. As co-workers we attempt to team up with them, and encounter difficulties. As we come to be leaders we attempt to manage groups, and we find that some groups work well and others are ineffective. And then when we initiate a major organizational change process, we encounter powerful resistance.

Why Groups Today?

Why are we so focused on groups and teams today? They have existed since the first hunting party left the cave. But in the organizations of the 1990s, teams and groups are critical. These teams don't need to be in a room together to accomplish common work. In fact, technology has created types of groups which never even existed in the past. They can now operate together or apart, in four basic scenarios:

	Same time	Different time
Same place	Traditional face-to-face meeting	Work-sharing
Different place	Teleconferencing	E-mail and voice-mail

As cost-cutting measures lead to a paring-down of the workforce, groups have become more important to organizations: we have fewer people trying to accomplish more. We can no longer afford to encourage each individual to specialize in one narrow area of operation.

Good and Bad Groups

There's a coach in one of the major leagues who was asked why he didn't put together a booster club for his team. The answer was simple: "I don't see the sense in putting together a group that's going to be after my head in three years."

It is an unfortunate reality that anything that has great power to help your business when done right also has great power to harm your business if done badly. So while groups can be enormously beneficial to business today, they can also be enormously destructive. Precisely because of their empowerment, groups can be major resisters of change.

They can have great synergy; this is the reason why small groups, representing minority opinions, can have such influence on the public and on policy-makers in a democratic state. As a leader, you must acknowledge group power, anticipate the group's thoughts and accept and recognize their validity; by so doing, you can forestall uprisings. If you include groups in the decision-making process and share information openly, you will have a stronger chance to gain their commitment to your vision.

Groupcount versus Headcount

How can you be sure that you're addressing groups appropriately? One fascinating approach is to perform a diagnostic test. Count the number of groups in your organization — groupcount rather than headcount. Can you do this? Are you even aware of what constitutes groups in your organization? (Careful — they aren't packaged in nice neat departmental boxes.) Groups have hierarchies and relative status in the organization. Groups can form by task, culture or interest. Performance management can be effected along any of these group lines, with bonuses for group achievement.

The acknowledgment of the contribution of groups has taken us outside traditional views. The progression has been something like this:

Old view: Do a headcount inside the organization. *Current view:* Acknowledge and empower teams or groups within the organization. *Coming view:* Recognize groups and teams across and beyond the web, encompassing strategic partners, suppliers and customers.

This is a dramatically new way of looking at organizational and group behavior and composition. It's comparable to the change in worldview when the Ptolemaic view of the universe, with the earth at the center, was finally ditched in favor of the Copernican system with the earth as just one orbiting entity. The organization is no longer at the center of its universe.

If your organization has been operated traditionally until now, your people will not be skilled at group work. Because the change process should ideally start with a team-building effort, you will need group output, and quickly. Going back to our first experiences in groups, remember that neither in the family setting nor in the school system do we receive group-skills training. What we learn in those settings we learn rather informally, although this information stays with us for life. If we encounter unpredictability — perhaps one parent had a quick temper — we learn never to speak up. If we encounter competitiveness in school, we will find it difficult to share knowledge openly with our peers, and we won't feel rewarded by facilitating their success. Much acquired behavior has gotten in the way of the simple sharing concepts we may have understood as very young children.

Your groups have to overcome the barriers set up

in previously learned behaviors. Classic individual motivators are achievement, power and affiliation — although not everyone is motivated by affiliation. Those motivated by personal achievement and individual power will have to be helped, through group-skills training, to supplement their natural motivation.

Crossfunctional teams toss out the traditional power structure and norms. We need to pay attention to that. We must not expect people to snap back to their old roles once the group's one-time task or objective has been completed. After you've taught them to get improved results in a new way, don't expect them to return to traditional methods. You wouldn't, and neither will they.

Managers often want to move toward a more participatory style, but are frustrated because people just won't speak up. It takes time to shift through changes. The difficulty is that few leaders achieved their promotions for their group-building skills. In fact, leaders are more commonly independent thinkers; classic leaders are *not* typically group or team players, however often they use these words. But being the leader of a competitive organization today is entirely about building teams and linkages, both internally and externally. This will be an essential skill for leaders of the 1990s and beyond. Only the leader can ensure collective input and consensus.

Similarly most senior management groups are still struggling to find a common purpose. Unless a group has articulated a sense of purpose, it will not last. But groups who do support a shared purpose are powerful agents for change and can be used by leaders in support of their change process.

POP QUIZ:

Creating Your Own Who's Who

One useful exercise is to assess your stakeholder support and identify those groups which are actively for, actively against and neutral to change. The area to invest your energy in, as leader, is the neutral contingent, particularly informal groups (the social committee, for example) which have huge invisible power in most organizations. Informal groups, by definition, come together for a particular reason, and thus have a strong sense of purpose — which may explain why your annual golf tournament is better organized than your energy-saving program. Informal groups also have the most emotional power (see chart below). In dealing with permanent informal groups, the leader must identify them, pay attention to them, and be as open as possible with them.

Make a list right now of your organization's temporary, permanent, formal and informal groups. Which are positive, negative and neutral?

A final question: who do you need to get on board next?

Figure 4 — Types Of Groups

	Temporary	Permanent
Formal	Task force for a particular purpose established in advance Experimental team with a specific purpose	Organization's "groupcount" Self-managed work teams Customer-focused work groups
Informal	Self-formed group to address a perceived problem	Self-created informal groupings Support staff, cafeteria groups, sports teams Rumor mills: potentially destructive

Most often, organizations are set up to motivate and reward individuals. But we can agree that groups have credibility, we can acknowledge that they have a purpose, and we can think about motivating and rewarding each group. We must remember though that not all groups are necessarily teams. NATO is a group of more or less equal members, not a team whose members have individual tasks.

MANAGEMENT TIP:

Groupwork

It is useful to recognize the common group lifecycle:

a. Individuals collect. There are unvoiced issues.
b. There is conflict over power and influence and roles within the group.
c. Consensus on process is reached — how to deal with beefs; ways of operating; how to have effective meetings; who will have which roles.
d. The group turns to getting the job done.

If you want a group to work, you must *enable* it to work, or it will most assuredly enable itself in proceeding through these stages. At first, most people want to dispense with (a) through (c), being impatient to get at the task; but in fact the first three steps are a good investment of time, causing the process itself to deliver a more effective result; don't try to jump over these crucial steps. Many groups, and almost all leaders, deny or ignore the importance of steps (a) through (c). All groups must meet from time to time, even if only electronically. They must have efficient ways of accomplishing tasks; they must achieve a common understanding. Remember, "process" is not a four-letter word! Taking time to agree on procedures is most difficult for "Type A" leaders — authoritative, top-down managers, but the stage is essential for good teamwork.

> "In some plants, we have no plant manager. An eleven-person team has responsibility for the factory process; they are responsible for measuring and improving our capability. The team decides how to adapt to strategies and creates its own agenda. Everyone has to know how to do everyone else's job, and the role of team leader rotates each month among team members. The team gets excited about finding ways to run the plant a little better all the time: it engages their competitive spirit to beat previous records, invent new changes, or apply new technology. I believe this is the answer for the future; the productivity improvement is incredible."
>
> SIR NEIL SHAW, CHAIRMAN AND CEO, TATE & LYLE PLC

Harnessing the Power of the Group

When players come to groups that extend beyond the organization, they come with their former group cultures and fears. A sense of affiliation and connectedness gives the group its energy and synergy. Change can threaten groups with a sense of loss of this affiliation.

We must recognize that people give more loyalty to groups than to organizations (like putting your family before your employer). Individuals know their groups better than they know their organizations. For groups, restructuring can feel like losing family rather than just losing (or changing) a job.

At the same time, we know that people have the ability to affiliate with different groups at the same time — you are at once a member of your church, your bridge club, your aerobics class and your political party. One way of retaining a sense of stability within an organization that is undergoing change, then, is to affiliate individuals with as many different groups as possible; they can retain a sense of normalcy by psychologically holding onto the stability of groups that stay the same, while other groups are disbanded or drastically changed.

Formerly, leaders saw themselves as leaders of individuals and learned many techniques for motivating them. Now, when we lead groups, the same techniques can be employed. It seems difficult for leaders to deal with groups, as opposed to either individuals or the organization as a whole. The leader must impart a sense of purpose and accomplishment to the group, and foster group recognition and self-esteem.

You don't want to break the synergy of a group, you want to harness it. To do so, you need to understand where the groups in your organization are headed; they may not be going in the same direction as you, or even as each other. They may be headed for disaster, or for a different but no less effective tangent from yours.

Team-building

Only the leader can build a group of individuals into a committed team.

- Let people know that you are interested in building a team and not just assembling a group of individuals. Do not speak in abstract terms. Describe what kind of team you want and how it will look.
- When you see people or groups of people seizing opportunities, acting hopeful and being curious, applaud their efforts. Share these incidents with the rest of the organization.
- Keep in mind that you and your management team do not need to resolve every problem on your own. When issues are raised, invite employees to deal with the problem. Solicit their efforts.

"Some groups will feel that the change is not in their best interests. Look for heroes in the group that have led change successfully, and make them feel that these changes can lead to a good conclusion. Involve groups early in the process. Some will resist for all sorts of reasons and be very negative. You need to keep building a critical mass of supporters of change, increasingly isolating those against it."

MARY ANN CHAMPLIN, SENIOR VICE-PRESIDENT

AETNA HUMAN RESOURCES, AETNA LIFE & CASUALTY COMPANY

MANAGEMENT TIP:

Going after groups (before they go after you)

The most dangerous group is one which is against you but is conforming, appearing to go along, while fostering covert rebellion. The solution to this problem is a multi-channel approach:

1) Work with the individuals within the group, identifying key influencers. Understand their objections to the change, and deal with those directly. Is their objection a valid one? Can it be dealt with another way?

2) Perform group-level interaction, fostering open communications and dialogue with the group. You may need outside help to get the group members to articulate their feelings about and understanding of the change.

3) Understand that the group has a particular objective which is forming the source of the problem. Try to meet the group halfway; negotiate a solution; give it a role on the positive side.

4) If all else fails, dismantle the group or change the players. Whenever even one person changes in a group, the group changes.

Above all, when encountering resistant groups, remember that those resisting are not always wrong. Listening can sometimes help you avert a looming disaster.

Letting Go of Competition

Communications, not just between individuals constituting groups but from one group to another, are essential today. Groups, particularly crossfunctional teams, will necessarily interrelate. For example, the team looking at performance measurement systems will ideally share ideas and information with another group created to look at rewards and incentives. Unfortunately, both the educational system and the traditional organizational structure have tended to support high levels of competitiveness among groups (most firms we know explicitly or implicitly encourage competition among regional sales groups, for example). The competitive model is largely based on hiding information from the competing group, and forcing each party to "guess" what is really going on.

We must give up this competitive model if we are ever to form successful strategic alliances, either within or outside the organization. There is no magic method to dissolve those competitive feelings, but education, particularly games and role-playing, can help people let go of the old behaviors and attitudes.

CHAPTER NINE

Changing One Mind at a Time

People have to care

·

Lessons from POW camps

·

By finding meaning in life,
they found meaning in work

·

"Let's vote on what the CEO is saying"

·

The evolution of organizations

·

When buy-in doesn't work

"Would You Buy a Used Vision from This Man?"

I can't tell you the name of the company. It's up in the top, say, 50 of the Fortune 500 list. And I can't tell you the name of the man. I wish I could; he's one of my heroes. He's a vice-president.

He's a quiet man, slow-spoken, and I've never seen him speak with his brow unfurled, even when he tells a joke.

He told me once that he'd made a speech at a company sales conference in Las Vegas — even though sales wasn't his department. The sales support team for the conference had provided the speech — a kind of visionary fluff more often delivered than believed. They'd also provided (1) a speech coach, (2) a background videotape, (3) a pyrotechnician to set off fireworks when he came to the part where the new corporate vision slogan was announced and (4) a baby elephant to drive the point home.

I'm lying about the baby elephant. It wasn't a baby elephant. But it was something just as overwrought.

He'd tried to rise to the occasion. He'd rehearsed, listened to his coaches, synchronized his delivery with the backup videotape and the fireworks and even made friends with the elephant. He'd smiled, used body language, ripped off his tie in the middle of the speech and yelled out the visionary slogan.

The meeting was videotaped for dealers who couldn't make it to the conference.

Two weeks after the meeting, he sat down and watched the videotape. "I looked like a bad game-show host," he said.

These days he has a little piece of paper taped to the inside of the middle drawer of his desk. It's handwritten and reads "Would you buy a used vision from this man?" He says he takes a peek at it every time he's tempted to go the easy route of selling the Leader's vision with hype, not heart.

He actually does very well at selling the vision in his

quiet way. He keeps everlastingly at it, persuading, repeating, cajoling. He paraphrases Lyndon Johnson on his reason for doing so: "You want them inside the tent peeing out, rather than outside the tent peeing in."

"Lasting improvement does not take place by pronouncements or official programs. Change takes place slowly inside each of us and by the choices we think through in quiet wakeful moments lying in bed just before dawn. Culture is changed not so much by carefully planned, dramatic and invisible events as by focusing on our actions in the small, barely noticed, day-to-day activities of our work."

PETER BLOCK, *THE EMPOWERED MANAGER*

Why Achieving Buy-in is No Easy Job

Buy-in. It's a concept that we use often in organizations and it means, simply put, that people have bought the story; have bought the dream; have signed on; are onboard. We have a number of different ways of expressing buy-in. For some, the problem is that buy-in means that, if individuals buy something, then somebody had to be selling it to them.

As we move from hierarchies to horizontal, webbed organizations, there will be less selling than telling, and more of a coming to an understanding. However, there will always be a place for leadership; and in this new framework, leadership will be selling ideas. That is why we have chosen to continue to use the term buy-in.

In the old days, buy-in looked something like this: the CEO gave a speech, primarily to large groups, that was videotaped and sent out to all of the offices and branches; sometimes it was used, sometimes it was not. Responses ranged from "Oh, that's where we're going. That's interesting. Nice to see the CEO," to "Who cares?" To achieve *real* buy-in, people have to care. People have to believe that the concept or strategy that's being sold is something *that they want to do*. They must personally want to make a contribution. People must feel that they can successfully add value, and understand how they might be able to participate.

It may not even be clear, immediately, precisely how they will contribute. The real goal for the leader is to win from the employees the desire, the wanting to, the belief that change needs to happen; that it can happen. Some people will only buy in, however, if they do understand in a less ambiguous way what their role will be. They are slower to commit. If we use a shopping analogy, they are the ones who shop for price, shop for value, shop for quality. They go to a number of different stores, they may have to see the product several times, and they insist on examining it in detail.

There are other employees, who, because of their nature, are more impulsive shoppers. They're with your organization, they want to do a good job, they like and believe in the leader, so they go for it.

There are dangers, however, in both extremes.

With the impulsive buyer, if they get the product home and if it doesn't work, their disappointment is huge because they were so caught up in the concept, they believed so much that it would contribute and bring something positive to their lives. If it doesn't, that disappointment will eat away at them; it will certainly eat away at any chance of ever their buying a similar product. They may even wonder if they should ever use that store again.

With the careful buyers, the downside is that the buy-in process will take more time. You can't just "get on with it" quickly. You will have to provide the data, the multiple visits, the multiple media, to get at them, and they may still not be sure. You'll have to work hard to find a way to get them to pick it up and try it.

In the past, CEOs primarily focused on the first type of employees, the ones who bought the idea quickly. Those who didn't buy it impulsively were basically disregarded as resisters, "not suitable for here," people who just didn't understand. It became very much a blaming process: if some people didn't buy in, didn't see the magic, it was their fault.

But achieving individual buy-in is the leader's job, the leader's responsibility. What could be more important than getting 50,000 people to believe and understand what needs to be done? Is it more important to go back and review the financials? Is it more important to, as we used to say, "go back to work?" There is nothing more important than having an impact on every individual. Why? Because then all of the hours, days, months and person-years being worked in that organization are aimed toward the same thing, and your employees' differences and creativity are adding value.

It may sound silly that I have to convince leaders that this is an important role. "Of course," they say, "that's important." However, what I see in practice is very different. There are lots of assumptions that people have bought in, and sometimes even a refusal to believe that people have not.

In the *Harvard Business Review* article "Changing the Mind of the Corporation," by Roger Martin, the author introduces the idea of "disrupted feedback." Many times, as consultants, we go out and provide leaders with information from focus group data, interview data and survey data that essentially tells them that people have not bought in. There is a tendency for leaders to want to explain away these data, to be angry at the lack of buy-in and to blame others for not coming on board. However, once leaders truly believe that this is their job, that it can be achieved, even if it takes one year or three to achieve it, they will have found a completely different priority in how they work.

Past Experiences Contribute to Present Reactions

Why is achieving buy-in so difficult? We have noted the different ways people buy, and the different methods and data they require, but there is a second factor that is just as important as style. The second factor is that people come with experience. They can have good experiences and bad, and mostly a mixture of both. But those experiences will tell them whether they really can trust the purchase of this idea.

Sometimes these experiences have taken place inside your organization. Sometimes they have come from other corporations and if the trust has been broken in the past, the resistance, the lack of willingness to sign on, to be part of the team, will be ingrained. In fact, we have today a whole host of organizations, and countless individuals who are cynical.

What does being cynical really mean? It means disbelieving: "Sure, tell it to me again. Sell it to someone who believes you." Where did this disbelief and cynicism come from? Were people born with it? No, it arose out of their past experiences. It may have started as early as their childhood experiences. The literature now available on the adult children of alcoholics helps us understand what growing up in an inconsistent, unpredictable and painful environment can mean. They provide examples which illustrate how one childhood lesson can influence an individual's willingness to buy in. For example, imagine that a child growing up in an alcoholic family is promised a trip to the park on Saturday. The child is excited, hopeful. Then Saturday arrives, and the park visit is forgotten. The child feels let down and disappointed. Now imagine that this childhood experience is repeated many times — although once in a long while the promised outing does take place. As the pattern is repeated time and again, especially in an inconsistent reinforcement pattern, behavioral psychologists such as B.F. Skinner tell us, the cynicism becomes increasingly ingrained, and there becomes disbelief that anything will really happen.

Let's take that to the organizational level. Isn't the pattern similar to what has happened in organizations through the last couple of decades? We have made promises as leaders. We may even have been sincere. But the promises were hard to fulfill: the shareholders wouldn't support us; the economy turned down; there was a global restructuring; our product cycle was late.... We promised, and then we failed to deliver. More often than not, we didn't keep our promise because we didn't think through what that promise meant, how hard it would be to keep and how much effort it would take from us as leaders to make the change. Some of us drop out of the marathon before the race is won; but unfortunately we've told a lot of people that we are going to run. We've gotten a lot of help and support from our people, and it is their disappointment that we have to deal with now.

To get through to people, then, knowing that each individual's experience is different, we must think about the type of communication, the type of honesty and sincerity, that it is going to take from us to gain trust and individual buy-in. We must think about what the job *means* — to every single person in the organization.

Finding Meaning

"One should not search for an abstract meaning of life. Everyone has his own specific vocation or mission in life to carry out a concrete assignment which demands fulfillment. Therein he cannot be replaced, nor can his life be repeated. Thus, everyone's task is as unique as is his specific opportunity to implement it."

VIKTOR E. FRANKL, *MAN'S SEARCH FOR MEANING*

Values are changing in the working world and, as never before, people must find meaning in their work. The leader's vision and the change process itself must create meaning for working people. Why must we provide meaning? People are cynical today in their dealings with their employers, skeptical, at times even hopeless. They no longer feel that they will find meaning in their company or work.

The leader's job is to link meaning to jobs. It's hard to find meaning and purpose without the dream. Meaningful work is a combination of the leader's vision and individual's own sense of purpose; both elements are necessary. People need to feel that their lives are meaningful in order to carry on living as well as working. The work and life of Victor Frankl have shown that, in the prisoner-of-war camps of World War Two, those who found a purpose in their suffering were those most likely to survive. The "New Age" movement of the eighties was an attempt to find meaning and purpose in our lives, in a time when the traditional religions were waning. One of the reasons people need meaning in their work now as never before, is that they have the luxury to deal with it; for most working people, just staying alive or finding enough to eat is no longer the central challenge. "Meaning" is having your needs met for where you are right now.

But you have to have a solid idea of what "meaning" is before you can hope to help your workers find it through their work.

There is a wonderful book called *What Color Is Your Parachute?*, by Richard Bolles, that contains a number of exercises to help people examining their career choices determine first what kind of life they want to lead. The idea is that people's passion for their own personal vision drives their efforts to restructure their work life to meet their personal needs. Read the book and do the exercises and you will see how large a part meaning plays in motivating change.

Now pass the book on to your executives.

Or try this: make a list of all the places you've ever worked — include paper routes and babysitting. Now ascribe a happiness quotient to each working experience on a scale of 1 to 5 (1 being hell and 5 being bliss). Don't think too hard about it, go with your first impression. Go back and look at the work situations that brought you the most happiness. Do they have anything in common? I bet pay levels have very little to do with how much you enjoyed yourself. I bet your happiness had everything to do with the people you worked with, how you worked together and your part in helping the group meet with success.

Meaning has to come from the inside out. In an organization, it usually comes from the outside in: mission, goals and so on. The only way to reverse the process is for people to understand inside-out what is important for them. When people don't have meaning in their work it's because they haven't identified "what's in it for me." It is necessary to make a personal connection with a personal vision, one's purpose in life.

"Only a company with a real mission or sense
of purpose that comes out of an intuitive or spiritual
dimension will capture people's hearts. And you must
have people's hearts to inspire the hard work
required to realize a vision."

JOHN NAISBITT AND PATRICIA ABURDENE, *RE-INVENTING THE CORPORATION*

An example can be found within People Tech. My vision statement for People Tech is very straightforward: "To help organizations do more than they ever thought was possible." This vision arises out of my belief in my own purpose for living: to help others to achieve their personal best.

We must overcome the notion that there is no place for the spiritual side in business. The way that we connect the two is to relate the life purpose to the business purpose. It is necessary for all individuals to take stock of how they got where they are and where they want to go. At People Tech, we want all leaders and change agents within our client organizations to go through this process before we complete an engagement.

We also believe that it is important for every employee to complete self-discovery exercises, not just the management team. You may be thinking: "How can we possibly get everyone through this? That's totally unrealistic!" But consider that self-discovery programs are just as important, and just as feasible, as your ongoing commitment to get every employee through training, health and literacy programs that your organization may be running. Yes, it can take a long time, but that does not mean it isn't necessary.

> "Work is irreducible. We don't work for food gathering or tribal power and conquest or to buy a new car and so on and so forth. Working is its own end and brings its own joy; but one has to have a fantasy so that work can go on, and the fantasies we now have about it — economic and sociological — keep it from going on, so we have a huge problem of productivity and quality in our western work. We have got work where we don't want it. It's an instinctual laming. And this is psychology's fault: it doesn't attend to the work instinct."
>
> JAMES HILLMAN, *A BLUE FIRE: SELECTED WRITINGS*

Fifteen years ago I worked on an engagement with The Cooperators, a major national insurance firm. At that time they were experiencing high turnover, and a reluctance among employees to make lateral moves. Working with a change management team, The Cooperators launched a ten-year career-planning process which encompassed every leader in the firm. The company invested one week in each individual, and assigned peer mentors to the process. Every employee completed a life's-purpose exercise.

After the first three years of this process, lateral moves tripled, retention soared, attrition was down. People also changed more than their jobs: they reported that their personal relationships improved, they undertook health and fitness programs and generally felt happier. By finding their meaning in life, people found meaning in their work. The process continues at The Cooperators today.

The business case for undertaking a program like this is simple. If you were to total up the hours management spends herding and prodding people, as opposed to equipping them to leap and run ahead, the extra hours would add up to a needless waste of time, talent and money. Understanding the passions that drive your life will inevitably make you happier and energize your work.

> "When we think of work, we only consider function and so the soul elements are left to chance. Where there is no artfulness about life, there is a weakening of soul. It seems to me that the problem with manufacturing is not a lack of efficiency, it is a loss of soul.
>
> THOMAS MOORE, *CARE OF THE SOUL*

It is difficult for most people to share their purpose in life with others; they are shy, afraid of being judged. That's why it is equally important to try to create an environment of mutual respect, in which people feel free to share their hopes and dreams. If such environments became the norm for business, there would be far greater understanding among groups and within the organization generally.

By the same token, most people are afraid to ask for help; they think that people won't respect them if they show vulnerability. In reality, we have learned that people do in fact respect those who ask for help; it gives the askers the opportunity to enroll others to their purpose. Imagine, for a moment, a business norm in which people always shared openly their hopes for accomplishment. That truth telling would be so powerful it could change the world.

MANAGEMENT TIP:

Seeing is believing

Visualization techniques, which have been so successful in the sporting world, are equally useful at work. Psychologists have learned that the brain does not distinguish our inner thoughts and feelings from objective, external reality. If we see something happening in our minds, it is as though it has happened in fact: the mind is incredibly powerful. Take the time to study visualizations and practice visualizing where you want your company to go.

Big dreams are a core part of what we are as humans. All evolution, seen from a certain perspective, is about overcoming obstacles and challenges; the fittest and most adaptable survive. We believe that human beings need a big vision, an impossible dream, to reach for as part of our evolutionary process. John F. Kennedy's call to "put a man on the moon and return him safely within ten years" galvanized the imagination of the world and motivated massive technological development which had ramifications far beyond the space program. We may have had the tools and technologies, but it was the big, then-impossible vision which gave shape to all subsequent activities.

Once your executives are done with *What Color Is Your Parachute?*, have them pass the book on to the front-line workers. Give the workers two hours a week to go through the book — I'll bet a number of them will take it home, because the process of self-discovery is so enticing. Ask them to deliver a report on their findings under the heading: "My preferred working environment is . . .". Now that you have an idea of what people are looking for from their jobs you can look for ways to incorporate and tie their visions to that of the organization.

The Three Types of Individual Orientations

Each individual has goals and a private agenda. It is

the leader's task to network people into groups. We must continue to recognize individuals as unique, with their own expectations.

Individuals can be described by three basic types — learners, task-dependents or people-dependents. Their responses to change differ widely.

Learners are early adopters of change. They have less fear and resistance to change than most others. They are prepared to try something new. On the downside, they will often make mistakes, and lose self-esteem in the process.

Task-dependents focus on doing what they are meant to do. They will do their job well, and quickly. In respect to change, they will have to clearly understand the need to change their task. They will find it hard to cope with personal change.

People-dependents go to work in order to socialize (this is not meant in a derogatory way). They are good delegators; they love helping others perform well. They know how to get the job done through people. These types have an emotional response to change. On the positive side, they are able to buffer change for other people. However, they are less likely to be able to connect to an intellectual, business case for change.

MANAGEMENT TIP:

Renegotiating your contract

To lead change is to renegotiate implicit contracts. This assumes that you have already discovered the meaning of change for yourself. Thus the process is:

1) The meaning of change must be discovered by the leader.

2) The leader needs to lead a change effort that helps people discover and renegotiate their implicit contracts with the organization, and find meaning in the change.

3) The new vision must ultimately take precedence, and some may not be able to discover the meaning and will need to leave.

About Conformity and Commitment

Conformity means acting in accordance with the wishes, real or perceived, of others. Conformity is a common tactic used by groups and group members undergoing change. Individuals also sometimes conform because of pressure from others. They may even demonstrate change as long as the pressure is on, but backslide quickly once the pressure is off. Our dieter shows up at the health club (and swims a few leisurely laps), orders the diet plate when dining out with friends (and stops off on the way home for ice cream and donuts), but has not truly changed. The essence of conformity is that external behavior is divorced from internal thoughts and feelings. Conforming behavior is always disappointing in group and organizational change. What is wanted is commitment, the enthusiastic pledge of the whole self.

"Commitment" is one of the hot words in business today. It means the same thing as buy-in. Unfortunately, up to 80% of companies are in danger of failing to achieve their strategic objectives because they can't tell the difference between an employee who is truly committed and one who has been scared into conforming but remains unconvinced.

Conformity is comfortable. You can hardly expect workers who have long found safety and solace in conforming to the rules of the organization to give them up overnight. Their success so far has been based on their ability to conform. They may, in fact, consider conformity and commitment to be the same thing. The difference between the two come down to this:

Conformist: "I'll do what you want."
Committed individual: "What I want to do is be part of what you are doing."

If we examine how organizations have evolved since the turn of the century, a clear pattern emerges. According to futurists Craig Hickman and Michael Silva, in their book *The Future 500*, there has been a distinct rise in importance, from 1900 to today, in both individual fulfillment and organizational flexibility. From rigid, structure-based practices in 1910, organizational focus has transformed through the productivity drive of the 50s, the systems obsession of the 60s and the strategic planning of the 70s. The 80s were characterized by a deep interest in company culture and workplace innovation. The 90s organization is about leadership and empowerment, neither of which can be achieved without mutual commitment between the leaders (representing the organization) and the workers (who are most flexible and productive when feeling fulfilled as individuals).

There are ways to tell when your employees are committed to your strategic changes. One is to get out there and measure feedback immediately. (Why wait until your program has fallen on its face?) Recently, a major manufacturer we worked with did an employee survey within six weeks of the introduction of a major TQM initiative, to gauge commitment. The survey showed that employees were confident that they would be successful, and believed in the commitment demonstrated by the management team. They questioned whether the firm's performance measurement guidelines supported the new initiative effectively, and they also asked management to confirm that the company was committed to the initiative for the long term (beyond one year). This feedback enabled the company to make minor but significant adjustments, and to gain commitment by giving it.

How Will You Know When Your Employees Are Truly Committed?

- Typically, your people do more than they said they would. They not only meet and exceed goals earlier, but they come back and ask for higher goals, rather than coasting on their early success.

- Another sign of commitment is seeing employees apply the new approach to other areas of their work. In the same company in which we did the survey, the managers used the newly introduced TQM initiative to drive their annual budget process, a core business activity. This act — staking one's career on a newly introduced technique — is the greatest visible commitment any employer could wish for.

Detecting *lack* of commitment is much more difficult, because people are good at conformity. Managers attempting to implement new business transformation programs must help workers understand the difference between conformity and commitment and seek to build the latter. Observe your staff's behavior. Pay attention to what people do and say. In *doing*, as we've seen, the committed apply new techniques to other areas of their work; conformers appear to, but lack follow-through ("I know it's important, but I just don't have time for it!" is a classic conformer's line). In *saying*, conformers are given away by their silence or the "yes-but" stance from which they view the new idea. Conformers will listen to alternatives but not offer them. Committed people ask questions, have alternative suggestions when they disagree with an approach and generally engage in the discussions surrounding change. When groups cannot progress naturally from one stage to the next by commitment, they move forward, in a fashion, by conforming. This creates the appearance of change without the substance.

"Something happens when you get a very wide support base of employees involved in the change process. Change takes greater depth; it snowballs. If you think your leadership is aggressive on change, wait till individuals get hold of it. As a result of leading change, I have become a better listener. I am more in tune with the idea of empowering people; I rely more on suggestions and direction from others."

TOM MCKENNA, PRESIDENT AND CEO,

MOORMAN MANUFACTURING COMPANY

When Buy-in Doesn't Work

You may be asking the question "If I have done all I can do and someone is still not on board, resisting and sabotaging, what should I do at that point? Have I failed?" There will be some people who do not fit into your organization. They came for the wrong reasons, they were sold a bill of goods, the organization has changed and no longer suits their style or needs. For whatever reason, they do not desire to make the change and you cannot afford to retain them. However, in the "turfing" of those individuals, we must be aware that we do not need to damage their self-esteem. It is not the individual that you are rejecting, it is their fit (or lack of fit) with your organization. Supporting them, not only through traditional methods of out-placement but by helping them to understand why the fit isn't there and examining the kind of environments or organizations that might make them happier, is a more facilitative approach. Imagine if every organization did this. Then the individuals that came to us from other corporations would be less damaged, and less likely to bring their cynicism with them. It will take a long time for people to reach a common level of self-esteem. But picture the world if that actually happened: a world in which people felt good about themselves and really could determine where they could contribute most effectively.

"Some people will make it through change,
others cannot. You need to develop and share
the vision and strategy, set the mindset, and gain buy-in.
Then people define their own role in the process.
Most people, at least 80%, are OK with change,
but some are not, and they eventually have to go."

EISUKE (ACE) TOYAMA, PRESIDENT AND CEO,

NISSAN CANADA INC.

Where Do We Go From Here?

CHAPTER TEN

Dear Dr. Change: Help!

Changeaholics and battle fatigue

·

The web and what to do about it

·

Wordism

·

The Cat in the Hat syndrome

·

How do we know when we're there?

Changeaholics

Q. I turned to face the changes — big changes — needed at my company about two years ago. Since then we have been retreating, benchmarking, partnering and changing our hearts out. The changes are producing results but I'm running out of steam. It takes so much energy that "getting up for it" is becoming more and more difficult. What can I do to stay fresh and enthusiastic about making these endless changes?

A. Sounds like you are suffering from battle-fatigue. The changes *should* be endless but your initiative should not be the only factor driving them. You have obviously equipped your people with some processes that will reveal where changes need to be made (as you have found through your retreats and benchmarking exercises), but you may not have given them the power or skills to drive the change themselves.

You want change to be endless, but you have to find ways of putting your workforce in the driver's seat so that you can pay more attention to the map and less attention to being a change agent. Right now, you are managing instead of leading. You have to abandon your managerial behavior if you want to empower your workers and teach them how to effect change themselves.

This is how empowerment works; start with your next change. Take one of your desired initiatives and assign it to a team. Make team members responsible for designing the plan to implement the initiative. Make them responsible for everything having to do with the initiative.

They should figure out who will do what, where the money will come from, what resources are needed and who to go to about getting them. Every time they come to you with a problem, ask them to come up with proposed solutions and then ask them which one they think will work. Insist that they coordinate with other teams in developing their plan by asking that a list of contacts accompany the plan. Let them decide if training or skill updating is necessary. Give them a deadline, a critical path and a headquarters.

When the plan is completed, circulate it among the contacts listed and pass it on to at least three other workers — at any level — who had nothing to do with the production of the report. Ask them to send their feedback to your E-mail. Once you've had a look at the feedback, send the plan back to the team and ask the members to implement it, incorporating the feedback as they see fit. Let them feel the risk and exhilaration of decision-making and change-driving that has taken the steam out of you.

Be absolutely firm — don't take responsibility back. If the team is having trouble knowing "what to do next," assign a human resources team to help them figure out what skills they need to meet their responsibilities. Give them all the support they need but don't decide anything for them.

Once your people become used to making change themselves, you will find a resting-place of sorts in the change process itself.

What a Tangled Web You Should Weave

Q. All of my company's teams work together. We have teams that partner on projects and a meeting of team coaches every couple of weeks. I've been describing the structure as a web to my colleagues in other organizations, but now I'm told my suppliers and customers should be part of the web as well. What exactly is a web structure and how does it work? You'd better tell me how I fit into it, too.

A. I like to view the web as a working environment that has been through a period of chaos and — through that chaos — has discovered a network of working relationships beyond the confines of the pre-chaos, boxy organization charts. *It is important to view the web as a growing, ever-emerging structure, and not as one that you impose on your company.*

The web structure includes the company's customers and suppliers as well as the employees and shareholders. Its boundaries are infinitely permeable and elastic. It can be likened to a tribe within which are a number of related clans; but newcomers can always join, unlike a traditional clan or tribe. All stakeholders are part of the web, whether or not they show up on your organization charts. The web acknowledges the interdependency of the relationships that affect work actions. Each strand of the web depends on others to support it.

Webs can be temporary or *ad hoc*. In Japan, industrial giants who are fiercely competitive in the domestic market cooperate to take on the world market. North American firms are still somewhat uncomfortable with this concept, but as major trading blocs form — NAFTA, EEC and Pacific Rim — companies within those blocs will increasingly cooperate in research, development, production and/or marketing. One example seen today is the cooperative agreement between computing rivals Apple and IBM to create a standard software platform that will accelerate the use of new applications and, presumably, increase the installed base of both firms' machines.

The web organization is one where leadership is at the center (see Figure 5). The power relationships are equal, and leadership is the glue that brings together partners (often known in the past as suppliers), paid employees and people outside of traditional corporate boundaries who are contributing to the mandate or the dream of the corporation.

What role do you play in this structure?

Leaders in the web must provide added value by initiating the learning, by increasing the dialogue; not by having all the answers. They help construct the belief system, bring out differences and work on consensus. They do not solve problems, they facilitate the move toward solving the problems.

Does this mean that leaders will never make decisions? Of course not. They will make many decisions. But many of their decisions will be around process: how do I bring people together? Who should be brought together?

Figure 5: The Webbed Organization

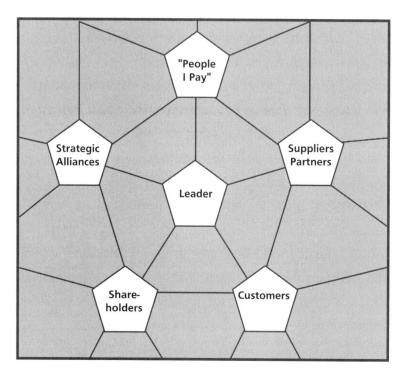

What's required from a learning framework? What do I need to learn in order to lead?

And leaders also have to replenish themselves. At one time leaders always had to be "on" and they always had to be right. They were known for their exemplary behavior, not for their learning behavior. In the web organization, leaders will always be learning. They will learn from family members, from neighbors, from the people they encounter day by day; they will be actively seeking insight and perspective.

"The leader needs a willingness to share, an openness.
You hear a lot about participative management in
which a manager shares information with his
subordinates. We don't hear however, about openness
among peers. There is still too much protecting of turf.
In future, we'll move beyond peers sharing information
openly to a point where we'll see companies openly
sharing with minority partners."

JOHN CASSADAY, PRESIDENT AND CEO, CTV TELEVISION NETWORK LTD.

Avoiding Wordism in Favor of Meaning (or, You'll Never Shift Paradigms in this Town Again)

Q. I was flipping through a training magazine the other day, reading the ads, and my mind just boggled at all the buzzwords. When is a change a paradigm shift? How many definitions of quality are there? I empowered myself and flung the magazine against a wall . . . but the words still haunt me. How much am I missing by not adding these terms to my vocabulary?

A. Please. Not knowing these terms is like missing a season of Beverley Hills 90210: you may not know who's dating Dylan, but when it comes right down to it, who the hell cares? These trendy turns o' phrase do little to enhance the understanding of the concepts they are based on. As a leader, you should of course be familiar with what it means to manage quality or change working patterns or help people do more than they ever thought possible. But many terms are more about fashion than about theory, and their continual reappearance only has the effect of disabling the language of management.

There is a theory about the use of words called the "plastic word theory" (by German linguist Uwe Porksen). It says that when words that are initially viewed as "specialized" or "scientific" come into popular usage, they eventually lose their power and become essentially meaningless. The following chart of buzzwords will help demonstrate the plastic word theory. Join any of the words on the right with any word on the left and, presto, a term is born. Join *any* word with any other word and the effect is the same.

Total	Quality
Instant	Success
Paradigm	Empowerment
Performance	Maximization
Support	System
Network	Development
Value-added	Benchmarking
Management	Leadership
Building	Communication (sad, but so true)
Virtual	Interface
Buy-in	Structure

Process	Flexibility
Pro-active	Service
Viable	Strategy
Integrated	Focus
Dynamic	Scenario
Critical	Initiative

You could bandy these words about all day and not say a thing.

And yes, I'm well aware that I have used some of these words in this book — but never without clearly defining what *I* mean by them — just as you should ensure that your workforce understands what *you* mean when you use terminology. Employing the right definition for a term is more crucial than employing the right word. Use a dictionary and look up the words on the chart above and you will reach a rounder understanding of the meaning behind this lingo. The phrase-coiners will forgive you and the world will be a better place.

The Cat in the Hat Syndrome

Q. "If it ain't broke, don't fix it" has always seemed to me to be an excellent adage. But the change theorists say that you have to shake things up a bit. It seems to me that there is a fine line between making changes and tinkering. Can you show me where it is?

A. In Dr. Seuss's story *The Cat in the Hat*, the cat in question gets a little spot on a dress. In an effort to get rid of the spot, he cleans the dress off in the bathtub, creating a mess in the bathtub. Every attempt the Cat in the Hat makes to clean up the mess results in a greater mess, until the whole house is a shambles. The Cat in the Hat was tinkering with cleaning up the mess, employing all the wrong tools for the job. If he had used spot remover and a washing machine to clean the dress, instead of the bathtub, the house would have stayed in order.

Likewise, while I advocate change I am not saying that any change will do. When I talk about creating chaos, I mean you are to create chaos where chaos is needed to develop a solution. Take a close, hard look at "what ain't broke" in your company; if the mechanism or process reflects forward thinking and isn't stale or so tightly bound by tradition that it *can't* work any other way, by all means leave it alone. Change is a prescription I give to organizations that are looking for new ways to work because the old ways aren't working or shortly won't work. In my experience, this describes the overwhelming majority of organizations.

If it ain't broke or ain't about to become ineffective, *don't* tinker with it. But *do* ask yourself why it's working what will make it keep working, and how you can make it work better. Undertake change as necessary.

By the way, what the Cat had *under* his hat were a

number of workers (known as X, Y and Z) who had the ability to clean up the entire mess in a matter of seconds. Would that we all had such creatures working for us. (Let me know if you find any.)

Technology and Elasticity

Q. I keep hearing about "business process re-engineering" these days. It sounds like some kind of technological "quick fix" — just add computers and stir. Isn't technology just being used to do the same old things faster?

A. Technology profoundly changes work; it doesn't just speed things up. After all, there is a limit to how fast things can go in the traditional ways of working. Think of the fax machine. True, it makes sending and receiving mail faster, but the changes don't end there. Visual information sent over the phone lines opens up a lot of new possibilities, and makes some older ways of working obsolete. What do you now receive over the fax that you never used to get by mail?

Business re-engineering is about using this power of technology in new ways. There are two kinds of business re-engineering, TQM and IT.

Total quality management (TQM). Looking at each process and making it better, alias the TQM movement, started in manufacturing and operations, and was prompted by Ford versus Japan in 1980. Seen initially as a means of avoiding error in manufacturing and operations, by the mid-1980s TQM had spread into planning and team issues, and it is generally defined today as "aligning people and process with customer satisfaction."

Information technology (IT). Organizations have looked to IT as a way to become more productive and profitable. However, technology solutions are incomplete, since they fail to recognize the human factor: they are not team-oriented or interpersonal.

"As for business process re-engineering," it can be described as "aligning people, process and enabling technology with customer satisfaction."

Examples abound of how these re-engineering processes have come together to influence and change organizations, particularly in the service industries. For example, the retail brokerage industry has changed substantially in the last five years. The source of power and influence inside these organizations is not hierarchical. They tend to be dominated by independent thinkers, brokers who have decided to have an association with a particular firm. Many of the more successful firms have changed from a task orientation — enacting stock transactions — to more of a service orientation, forming relationships with key clients and providing value-added advice and guidance. Those clients who just want transactions can use the new discount brokers. Technology too has supported and enabled this transition, facilitating automated transactions, 24-hour trading, and the use of databases to show brokers which customers might be interested in which new stocks through tracking their past preferences. The use of technology for governance in the financial sector — automated alarms if questionable trades are made or certain large orders seem suspicious — has had its effects on the industry as well.

Elastic boundaries between employer and employee are being seen in the brokerage industry, insurance and real estate; many firms are becoming loose associations of skilled people who come together under a certain banner and share values, as well as workspace and profits. Technology helps make this elasticity possible.

Relationships between supplier and customer have been especially facilitated by technologies such as electronic data interchange (EDI). Many suppliers now routinely allow their customers, such as manufacturing firms, to access their logistics systems directly. Thus a manufacturer waiting for a parts order can track whether the parts have been made or shipped and can intervene if it needs to adjust the order to a different specification.

Business re-engineering, TQM and IT contribute to the web organization. Elastic boundaries, customer focus, networking, individual decision-making; these are replacing the familiar structures with "virtual organizations." For some people, the prospect is terrifying (computer geeks rule the world); for others it is liberating (time and space are finally under control). However, not all organizations can disperse completely into microchips, although almost any business can learn something from the techniques of business re-engineering. Think about it: how are you using technology in your organization? Is it working for you or are you working for it?

We're on the Road to . . .?

Q. How do I know when we've "arrived"?

A. If you've been paying attention, you will know now that you never, ever, ever "arrive." The minute your organization starts to rest on its laurels, it will start developing hemorrhoids. The beauty of the ever-changing workplace is that it is not static. The responsive nature of the web organization makes change the one constant aspect of your working environment. Get comfortable navigating on the road, and keep the windows open to let the sweet smell of success waft over you as you and your team explore the routes you've mapped out. The model below shows why your road is an endless one.

Figure 6 — New Ways of Working

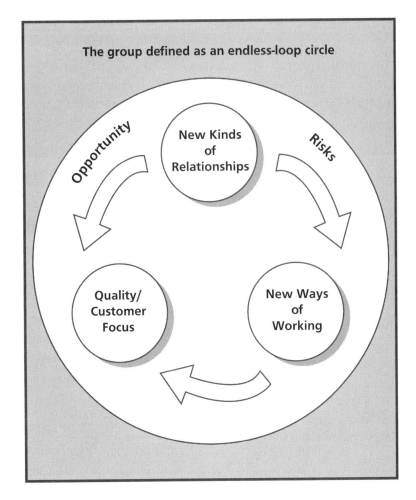

CHAPTER ELEVEN

Diversity

Using diversity to generate
better ideas

·

Access, process, outcomes . . . a more
diverse diversity

·

"Diversity is not easy to do
but it is easy to ruin."

ROBERT, BOB AND ROBBY have always worked
really well together as a product development team. The
boss has never heard a discouraging word uttered among
the three of them. They are all nice, bright, stable young
family men who have good taste in ties. They have come
up with an idea to develop a green squeeze-cheese snack.
Each takes the idea home to his son — ages nine, eight
and ten, respectively — and the boys agree that if such a
product existed they would demand that their mothers
buy it, and their mothers all agree that the product would
be just gross enough to work. Terrific. The team writes
up a proposal complete with a detailed marketing plan to
support the product, and the boss says: "Is this it?"

They nod their heads in unison.

"There's nothing so dangerous as one good idea. I need more than this. Back to the drawing board." So off they go, scratching their heads, trying to figure out what they've done wrong — everything was going so smoothly. . . .

The Value of Diversity

A homogeneous environment can be very comfortable. If all the people you work with are somewhat like you, they will tend to reinforce the validity of your belief systems and support your ideas. They know where you are coming from, they know where you've been — in fact, they've been there too (and had a terrific time). And snug in the warmth of your shared experience, you will all fail to relate to your global market — a diverse, messy, increasingly sophisticated and demanding batch of potential purchasers who won't understand green cheese (or *only* green cheese).

Most larger companies will tell you that they're interested in being global corporations and in developing "world products." A stroll through their head offices shows that the interest may not go beyond rhetoric. To be effective in a diversity of markets, corporations must be diverse. If you plan to develop new and exciting ideas for a particular market, that market ought to be represented in your workforce. The only thing that the three sons of the three Bobs can tell you is what sons of Bobs will buy.

The more backgrounds you bring to the decision-making table, the better the quality of the ideas you will develop. Your company will need quality ideas drawn from a diverse workforce to compete with those companies that are already seeing the benefits of diverse thinking on their bottom lines. Consider:

- Aetna Life and Casualty won praise (and free publicity) for its ability to service its Florida policyholders using Hispanic-American claims representatives during the aftermath of Hurricane Andrew.

- In a soft housing market, Bramalea Limited sold 80 out of 91 houses within one week, all in an elite market range. They were *feng shui* houses — houses designed to respect the traditions of the Asian market. *Feng shui* relates one's physical environment to one's spiritual life. Chinese buyers were attracted to the homes at the Noble House development by marketing materials which featured a peacock — the traditional symbol of fertility and success. Bramalea's Asian employees and its advertising agency's Asian art director helped guide the company to success.

- Insurance giant Cooperators Financial Services found that prospective customers made decisions based, in part, on how well they felt the company's employees and values mirrored their own. Input from Chinese-Canadian staffers was vital in the preparation and decoration of a new office in west-end Toronto which would primarily serve the Chinese-Canadian community.

• By the end of this century more than half of the North American workforce will be neither male nor white.

Your company's ability to maintain and increase its existing market share in a global marketplace will depend on developing and penetrating non-traditional markets. It is clear that no one person or group can understand the whole system. Systems thinkers call this the law of requisite variety: variety inside the system should be at least as great as environmental variety. As Karl Weik wrote, "If a simple process is applied to complicated data, then only a small portion of that data will be registered. . . . Most of the input will remain untouched and will remain a puzzle to people concerning what is up and why they are unable to manage it."

What Constitutes Diversity?
Diversity refers to more than ethnicity. Diversity also encompasses differences in perceptions, experience, patterns of speech and more. Marilyn Loden and Judy B.

Rosener, in *Workforce America,* describe the dimensions of diversity by two sets of parameters.

Primary dimensions which shape our self-image:
- age
- ethnicity
- gender
- physical abilities/qualities
- race
- sexual/affectional orientation

Secondary dimensions which we acquire, discard and modify as we develop:
- educational background
- geographic location
- income
- marital status
- military experience
- parental status
- religious beliefs
- work experience

At your next executive meeting, make a mental note of the similarities and differences in the backgrounds of the people at the table, using the above attributes to help guide you through your evaluation. If your respect for their opinions is based on their similarity to your own viewpoint, it is time to re-examine your decision-making criteria.

> "Incremental change is not enough for many companies today. Managers groping about for a more fundamental shift in their organizations' capabilities must realize that change programs treat symptoms, not underlying conditions. These companies do not need to improve themselves; they need to reinvent themselves. Reinvention is not changing what is, but creating what isn't. A butterfly is not more caterpillar or improved caterpillar; a butterfly is a different creature."
>
> TRACY GOSS, RICHARD PASCALE AND ANTHONY ATHOS

Managing Workplace Diversity

Fostering an atmosphere of mutual respect and tolerance in a diverse workplace is obviously a managerial challenge. The three Bobs might not work so smoothly with a Natasha or Rocko in their midst — but nor would they come up with green squeeze cheese.

The ability to serve a diverse community comes from changes in access, process and outcomes.

Access refers to developing and providing products and services which reflect the diversity of your customer base.

Do your products and services have attributes that

make them attractive to particular markets? Compare your newest products to the specific needs of the various communities you wish to serve. Make a list of whom you expect to use a certain product and, for each group on the list, come up with five ways to add value to that product which would serve that market's needs.

Process refers to how these products and services are developed. Power-sharing lies at the heart of the diversity issue.

Has your diverse workforce been given the power to suggest and shape the kinds of services you need to service your diverse market? Can the existing corporate structure respond quickly to such suggestions? At your next meeting, ask each person to describe what input they felt they had in the production of your latest product or service. Then ask them what they would personally do to enhance the product to make it "perfect" for use at home. *Their* homes. Encourage them to dream up a product that would suit the exact needs of their households. Now ask them why the product or service does not contain these elements (was it the expense or a lack of time, or was no one listening?).

Outcomes refers to envisioning the benefits of workplace diversity and working to see that they come to fruition. For visionary organizations, the aim of equity is not only to enhance participation, but to do more in the community — to make a positive contribution to creating social harmony.

What outcomes do you envision taking place in your diversified workplace? Answers to this question may include:

- increasing sales;
- enhancing customer service;
- building a more dynamic workplace;
- developing education and skills that are empowering;
- developing a compensation system tied to success;
- developing community outreach programs;
- enhancing competitiveness.

All these outcomes suggest managerial approaches, each a major undertaking. To ensure the success of diversifying your workforce, a leader has to have a clear picture of what that success would look like.

Try this: rank the above list of outcomes. Decide on your top three desired outcomes. Now indulge in a daydream of a diversified workplace. Try to see how these outcomes would emerge. It may help if you think of your workplace as the setting for a television show (you know, such as *L.A. Law*). On television, you can always "see" a plot developing. In creating your own plot to tie diversity to outcomes it may help to borrow some storylines from pop culture. On television shows, stories develop incrementally over a long period of time. Use the following outline to help:

Week 1: New characters are introduced to the work-place. They have each been brought in for a different reason. What are their assignments?

Week 2: They have met their co-workers, a couple of whom seem a little resistant to their new colleague. What has your company done to create a welcoming and supportive environment for the new workers? What has your company done to prepare the work-place for the entrance of these dynamic new people you've hired to make a difference for you?

Week 3: The new workers are settling into their positions and begining to show how they can contribute. What is your company doing to make sure their talents and competencies are revealed and put to use? Have you structured the workplace to give them the power they need to do the jobs you've hired them to do? Do their methods of work require an adjustment to the current working environment?

Week 4: It's been a month and the real contributions of the influx of new workers are beginning to become evident. Where are these contributions most evident in your company? How has their co-workers' work been over the last month? Has there been a noticeable difference in sales, morale, quality, the meeting of deadlines, service, idea contribution, new clients, new contacts, the "knowledge" of the company? What are the success stories of each of your new workers? What are the success stories of their collaboration with your existing workforce?

By "seeing" how you want the story to develop, you can create a route for success and even imagine the kinds of characters you need to play out the story. But always be ready for the unexpected twists that any change produces — you have to be ready to respond to the specific needs of your workforce.

Preparing for Diversity

Even today, we observe leaders who, while inviting healthy dissension and debate, subtly discourage anyone from speaking against the "party line." Conflict avoidance, "survivor" behavior resulting from constant downsizing, and uncertainty reign at all levels in most organizations, and the richness, breadth and depth of diverse ideas and opinions are often discounted.

Recently, People Tech developed a business game called *Every Kind of Person*. In developing the game, we conducted research to determine the measures of excellence which, if practiced, can be used to overcome barriers or challenges in valuing diversity.

In the game, like the real world, teams earn some

advantage by dealing with diversity effectively. Winning companies recruit to ensure that their workplace reflects their customer base. However, pro-active recruiting from among non-traditional applicant pools can lead to disproportionate clustering within an internal section or unit (usually corporate staff). This tends to work against diverse employees, as it can foster "we/they" attitudes. Active steps must be taken to avoid this polarizing practice.

Your own policies, procedures and requirements may also act as barriers to a diverse workforce. Screening for academic credentials is a traditional approach, but is not always an accurate process for assessing job-related skills. The seemingly neutral requirement of a university degree for many of today's jobs effectively screens out many persons with disabilities, women and people of color. Yet the actual duties of many jobs may not require a university degree to be well performed. Real-world experience teaches plenty.

If companies don't diversify voluntarily, it will be done for them. Equity legislation has been enacted in jurisdictions all over the world. The business sector complains that governments enforce equity clumsily, but as policy-makers they must respond to their constituency if businesses won't. Demographic trends are reflected in policy planning, and the world is changing whether your company is responding or not. Equity legislation is the manifestation of the state's responsibility to maintain and support social harmony.

Find diversity by:

- actively recruiting in high schools;
- offering training and education linked to achieving business strategies;
- offering scholarships and bursaries;
- using buying power to purchase from businesses owned by minorities and women-owned businesses;
- creating outreach programs to develop and maintain linkages to new communities;
- reflecting commitment to diversity within the organization.

Quite regardless of legislation, truly effective leaders are addressing the issues involved in diversity today — with an eye toward their bottom line.

CHAPTER TWELVE

Having Fun
and Looking Back

The nineties: fun forbidden

.

"No, I *have* to play now"

.

The myth of work . . .
the cost of not having fun . . .
the value of the person who's having fun

.

The journey so far

Come on. Get unserious

I don't know when it became socially unacceptable to have fun while you work. Gee, at one time even the guys working on the chain gang used to sing.

Look around the office. You see two people, each working at a computer. One has a light sheen of sweat on his/her brow. His/her lips are pursed. His/her eyes are as cold as Medicine Hat, Saskatchewan. The other is grinning and sort of bouncing up and down on the chair. Quick: which one would you give the raise to? Which one would most of your managers give the raise to?

So much for strength through joy in the workplace.

Did Lee Iacocca have more fun in his job than what-shisname — the guy who used to be the president of that other car company? Which of them accomplished more? Did Steve Jobs have more fun than just about anybody you could name at Big Blue? Do your employees have more fun than the people who work at your competition? And what are you losing if they don't?

At Nissan Design International Inc., they have a basketball court. They also have a sand volleyball court and a rooftop tennis court. And they have a workshop where employees can bring their families on weekends. Nissan is a serious company; just ask Volkswagen or General Motors.

You can't afford to wait for the economy to improve before you try to introduce fun into the workplace. Health, innovation and creativity flow from fun and are stifled by stress. Everyone knows that depressed, unhappy people get sick more often than people who are enjoying themselves. Workplace absenteeism caused by stress costs business billions of dollars in reduced productivity.

What do you think happens to the chain-gang productivity if you tell the guys to pipe down and get serious?

One person's fun is another person's afternoon in hell

During the research for this book, I got the following fax from a colleague in Seattle:

To: Marti and the team at People Tech

From: Wendy Potter

It's 7:30 p.m. after a gorgeous sunny day. My brain is soggy, but I'm halfway through the manuscript, first pass anyway. It's lonesome here by myself, but this is fun work. . . .

Now, to many of us, sitting in a library in Seattle on a sunny day would not be fun work. To others, skydiving, which some people enjoy, would be a nightmare. One of my colleagues once confessed that when she was planning a social event for her company, she found it stressful when she tried to think of fun skits.

We've all heard the stories about the creative geniuses at Apple Computer playing basketball in the atrium of the head office. Good for them, but what if you loathe basketball? And all those companies that give dinner dances? The people who love to dance have a rip-roaring time, the rest cower by the bar — or at home. Family picnics? Great for families, deadly for singles. Pep rallies? If you genuinely enjoy wearing a funny hat and yelling slogans, fine. But don't expect everyone to share your enthusiasm.

You are a leader, not a cruise director. ("Come along, Mrs. Finkelstein, of course you want to play shuffleboard.") You can't force fun on people, you can only provide the opportunities and the right environment and let people find their own fun. Don't haul them out of the library to put on skits if they are having more fun in the library.

What you can do is provide some facilities, and let your employees decide on how and when they want to use them.

- One company keeps a pingpong table in the storage area. The table was cheap, yet it is often used by the employees.

- A dartboard or a chess set in the lunchroom may encourage R&R during the day.

- Don't overlook the value of the lunchroom itself. Someone I know went from a company with a bright, cheery lunchroom to a company with a sink and a microwave in a dreary basement alcove, and she says it took her twice as long to get to know people at the second company.

- Meeting rooms with comfortable chairs, low tables and a blackboard encourage informal brainstorming sessions.

- Computer games built into the corporate software may help people recharge when they are getting stale.

- The very design and arrangement of the office can make a huge difference in the opportunities for meeting people and connecting. Does your interior layout encourage or inhibit chance meetings and places to group?

Fun is unpredictable and spontaneous, and there are as many different kinds as there are people in your company. Opportunities to gather on the spur of the moment are far more valuable than dozens of scheduled social events or sports teams.

Actually, social events and sports may have a hidden message: yes, we know the work here is mind-numbing, so we've decided to help brighten up your drab lives with a little laid-on festivity. Have fun — or else.

Shouldn't the fun be in the work itself? It's the last place people look for it, and it should be the first.

The myth of work

My brother is the successful CEO of a community bank in the midwestern United States. One Saturday he invited his son Joshua to come to the store with him. Joshua looked sad and said, "No, Dad, I have to play now." My brother realized that Joshua was unconsciously mimicking what he himself said when he went to work. Joshua would ask if they could play together and my brother would say, "No, Josh, I have to go to work now."

The attitude of "having to," of working to live, kills us. My brother is one of those people who really love their jobs, but his story illustrates how the idea of work as one thing and play as another is ingrained in us.

This is what I call the myth of work. Research by Mihaly Csikszentmihalyi, author of *Flow: The Psychology of Optimal Experience*, shows that although many people report that they feel dull or dissatisfied during their leisure time and get greater satisfaction from their work, they *still* say they would rather be doing something other than work! Why? It's a holdover from the industrial age, where work was a matter of survival and people were treated like machines.

A lot of people become more productive and make more money *after* they retire. I think this is because they don't associate what they were doing — writing a book, restoring antique furniture, inventing something — with work. We need to bring that attitude and experience into our lives before we retire.

Csikszentmihalyi developed a theory of optimal experience called "flow," which he defined as a state in which people are so involved with what they are doing that nothing else seems to matter. The experience itself is so enjoyable that people will engage in it freely, just for the sheer pleasure of doing it. Flow is the effortless state in which people's psychic energy is invested in goals that they have chosen to pursue. This is the "high" of work or accomplishment. We've all experienced it, more often at work than anywhere else.

Ultimately, this is what the web organization is all about. This is where change should lead you. It is at the root of teamwork and individual buy-in and reinventing yourself and your company. I started by talking about pain; I want to end by reminding you that you are working toward something much more than just the absence of pain. You are working toward flow (or fun, if you prefer to call it that).

Sure, the road leads through chaos and stress and uncertainty. There will be rough going; it's unavoidable. Some people may opt out. New people will shake things up. But one day — it will happen — you will find that a day at work has passed without your glancing at a clock or longing for the weekend. You may even find yourself whistling. Hey, it worked for the Seven Dwarfs.

Where we've come so far

Before you close this book, let's just look at where we've been. We started with the "ouch" of pain: who feels it, who should feel it and what it means. Pain is good, it's healthy. If you don't feel pain, you're dead. We started by hobbling a bit, but at least we started to move.

We scaled the change triangle and surveyed the three levels at which change must occur: the level of the organization as a whole, the level of groups within the organization, and the level of every single individual in that organization. Then we rolled up our sleeves and plunged in: making the case for change (not once and again, but again and again, and again and again and *again*). We shared the pain with everyone within earshot and kept at it, with fact and figures and workshops and group retreats and bigger and bigger whiteboards.

We met the four types of change management: top-down, cascade, network and cloning. We encountered strategic deciding, very different from strategic planning, and a rather frightening beast at first. Strategic deciding isn't linear and rational, it's chaotic and emotional, but it gets people involved right away.

We climbed up the five stages of change: ignoring, attending, planning, executing and embedding, and talked about relapses (*thump*) from one stage to another. This was so we would expect certain kinds of reaction and behavior and we wouldn't feel quite so frustrated when change took more time (and more repetition) than we thought it would.

We tackled the hurdle of reinventing the leader. We tried to break the news gently that all the things that got you where you are today have been preventing you from moving onwards and upwards. Getting on with change in your life and in the life of your organization means shedding some excess baggage. Some of it was hard to let go of, some (such as, perhaps, your ulcer medication) will never be missed.

Then we entered the realm of the sacred cows and the cult of the policies and procedures manual. Feel like Indiana Jones yet? Into the darkest corners of the human resources department, into the farthest reaches of the management information systems, up the meandering creeks of the financial department with or without a paddle. Nasty surprises lurk behind apparently innocuous traditions; they have to be brought squirming into the light and ruthlessly despatched. This is not a job for the squeamish or faint of heart.

Undaunted, we headed off to hunt down and corral the groups in the organization. Harnessing these creatures may feel like roping steers, but the energy of the groups can move the organization in the direction of change at a giddy rate. Just hang on and try not to lose your hat.

Finally, we took on the battle for the hearts and minds of everyone in the organization, from the VPs to the cleaning staff. It wasn't a loud or violent battle; it was quiet and sometimes quite invisible. Finding meaning in the job is different for every individual; no two people will ever do it in quite the same way. Here is where you have to be prepared to get up-close and personal; for some people this is the most terrifying job of all.

We paused to consider questions of battle fatigue and

the web organization. We tried to cut through the thickets of jargon (TQM, IT, business re-engineering, visioning, paradigm shifts and viable pro-active mission-critical integrated implementation-oriented . . . erm . . . something-or-others) to show that life is complicated enough without using polysyllables and acronyms to describe perfectly straightforward, commonsense ideas.

We paid a visit to the colorful land of diversity and learned about opening up the organization to new views and new voices. And we ended up with having fun (either sitting in a library or skydiving, one or the other, I forget which) and going with the flow. Fun is not just something tacked on to provide a cute ending to the book — it is the point of the whole exercise.

It's been quite a journey. Now all you have to do is repeat it all over again with your particular organization. Good luck — and don't forget to send us a postcard.

Notes and
Further Reading

Chapter 1

Summary of organizational trends adapted from "Paradigms for Postmodern Managers," *Business Week*, special issue on "Reinventing America," 1992, pages 62–63. See also David Jamieson and Julie O'Mara, *Managing Workforce 2000: Gaining the Diversity Advantage* (San Francisco: Jossey-Bass, 1991).

Chapter 2

Change model: Marti Smye and Robert Cooke, "The Key to Corporate Survival: Change Begins and Ends with

People," in *The Change Management Handbook*, Lance A. Berger and Martin A. Sikora, editors (New York: Business One Irwin, 1994).

Concept of time horizons: Elliott Jaques, *Time-Span Handbook: The Use of Time-Span of Discretion to Measure the Level of Work in Employment Roles and to Arrange an Equitable Payment Structure* (London: Heinemann, 1964).

Mental models: Pierre Wack, "Scenarios: Uncharted Waters Ahead," *Harvard Business Review*, vol. 63, no. 5, September/October 1985, pages 73–89. See also: Peter Senge, *The Fifth Discipline: The Art and Practice of the Learning Organization* (New York: Doubleday, 1990); Chris Argyris, *Overcoming Organizational Defenses: Facilitating Organizational Learning* (Boston: Allyn and Bacon, 1990); Arie P. de Geus, "Planning as Learning," *Harvard Business Review*, vol. 66, no. 2, March/April 1988, pages 70–74.

Alignment: Michael Beer, "Managing Strategic Alignment," in *The Change Management Handbook*, Lance A. Berger and Martin A. Sikora, editors (New York: Business One Irwin, 1994). The same idea is also known as "contingency" or "congruence": see Tom Burns and G.M. Stalker, *The Management of Innovation* (London:

Tavistock, 1961); Paul R. Lawrence and Jay W. Lorsch, *Organization and Environment: Managing Differentiation and Integration* (Boston: Harvard University Graduate School of Business Administration, 1967), pages 185–210; David A. Nadler and Michael L. Tushman, "A Model for Diagnosing Organizational Behavior," *Organizational Dynamics*, vol. 9, no. 2, Autumn 1980, pages 35–51.

Core competencies: C.K. Prahalad and Gary Hamel, "The Core Competence of the Corporation," *Harvard Business Review*, vol. 68, no. 3, May/June 1990, pages 79–91.

Response ability: see, for example, Edward E. Lawler III, *The Ultimate Advantage: Creating the High-Involvement Organization* (San Francisco: Jossey-Bass, 1992). See also Douglas McGregor, *The Human Side of Enterprise* (New York: McGraw-Hill, 1960) and the discussion of the work of Kurt Lewin in Marvin R. Weisbord, *Productive Workplaces: Organizing and Managing for Dignity, Meaning, and Community* (San Francisco: Jossey-Bass, 1987), pages 70–104.

Continuous learning: Peter Senge, *The Fifth Discipline: The Art and Practice of the Learning Organization* (New York: Doubleday, 1990). See also Dorothy Leonard-Barton, "The Factory as a Learning Laboratory," *Sloan*

Management Review, vol. 34, no. 1, Fall 1992, pages 23–38; David A. Garvin, "Building a Learning Organization," *Harvard Business Review*, vol. 71, no. 4, July/August 1993, pages 78–91; Daniel H. Kim, "The Link between Individual and Organizational Learning," *Sloan Management Review*, vol. 35, no. 1, Fall 1993, pages 37–50.

Chapter 3

Why employees don't: Ferdinand F. Fournies, *Why Employees Don't Do What They're Supposed to Do and What to Do about It* (Blue Ridge Summit, Pennsylvania: Liberty House Books, 1988). Each item on the list is the title of a chapter in this book.

Chapter 4

Network model: another term for the network is "transition team." See Jeanie Daniel Duck, "Managing Change: The Art of Balancing," *Harvard Business Review*, vol. 71, no. 6, November/December 1993, pages 109–118.

Cloning model: Michael Beer, *Organization Change and Development: A Systems View* (Glenview, Illinois: Scott Foresman, 1980).

Strategic deciding: Susan Dunn, "Creating a Learning Organization for Continuous Strategic Improvement" (unpublished paper, People Tech, 1994).

Strategic planning problems: Henry Mintzberg, *The Rise and Fall of Strategic Planning: Reconceiving Roles for Planning, Plans, Planners* (New York: Free Press, 1994).

Chapter 5

Stages of change: Wendy Potter, "The Stages of Change: A Theory and Model of the Process of Organizational Change" (unpublished paper, People Tech, 1993). This paper builds on the work of Kurt Lewin, who proposed three stages — unfreezing, movement and refreezing — in *Field Theory in Social Science* (New York: Harper & Row, 1946). Claes Janssen suggests four stages: contentment, denial, confusion and renewal; his work is cited in Marvin R. Weisbord, *Productive Workplaces: Organizing and Managing for Dignity, Meaning, and Community* (San Francisco: Jossey-Bass, 1987), page 266. Five stages in individual change have been identified by James O. Prochaska, Carlo C. DiClemente and John C. Norcross, "In Search of How People Change: Applications to Addictive Behaviors," *American Psychologist*, vol. 47, no. 9, September 1992, pages 1102–1114.

Senior management chasm: idea based on a "learning map" developed by Root Learning Inc. of Ohio.

Chapter 6

Difference between leaders and managers: Abraham Zaleznik, "Managers and Leaders: Are They Different?", *Harvard Business Review*, vol. 70, no. 2, March/April 1992, pages 126–135.

Three kinds of intelligence: other researchers suggest even more different kinds of intelligence. See, for example, Howard Gardner, *Frames of Mind: The Theory of Multiple Intelligences* (New York: Basic Books, 1983). Gardner mentions linguistic, musical, logical-mathematical, spatial, bodily-kinesthetic and personal intelligence, and suggests that there is no definitive list of the possible kinds of intelligence.

McKinsey: John Huey, "How McKinsey Does It," *Fortune*, vol. 128, November 1993, pages 56–81.

Management by walking around: The expression comes from Thomas J. Peters and Robert H. Waterman, Jr., *In Search of Excellence: Lessons from America's Best-Run Companies* (New York: Warner, 1982).

Chapter 7

Organizational systems: A related concept is organization archetypes and "frame-breaking change." See, for example, Royston Greenwood and C. R. Hinings, "Understanding Strategic Change: The Contributions of Archetypes," *Academy of Management Journal*, vol. 36, no. 5, October 1993, pages 1052–1081.

Chapter 9

Lasting improvement: Peter Block, *The Empowered Manager: Positive Political Skills at Work* (San Francisco: Jossey-Bass, 1987), page 189.

Disrupted feedback: Peter Martin, "Changing the Mind of the Corporation," *Harvard Business Review*, vol. 71, no. 6, November/December 1993, pages 81–94.

Vocation/mission and meaning of life: Viktor E. Frankl, *Man's Search for Meaning* (New York: Washington Square Press, 1984), page 131.

Personal vision: Richard Bolles, *What Color Is Your Parachute?* (Berkeley: Ten Speed Press, updated annually).

People's hearts: John Naisbitt and Patricia Aburdene, *Reinventing the Corporation: Transforming Your Job and Your Company for the New Information Society* (New York: Warner, 1985), page 22.

Work ethic: James Hillman, *A Blue Fire: Selected Writings* (New York: Harper & Row, 1989), pages 171–172.

Loss of soul: Thomas Moore, *Care of the Soul: A Guide for Cultivating Depth and Sacredness in Everyday Life* (New York: HarperCollins, 1992), page 183.

Evolution of organizations: Craig R. Hickman and Michael A. Silva, *The Future 500: Creating Tomorrow's Organizations Today* (New York: New American Library, 1987), page 247.

Chapter 10

Web organizations: for descriptions of new forms of organization, see Charles B. Handy, *The Age of Unreason* (Boston: Harvard Business School Press, 1989); John A. Byrne, "The Virtual Corporation," *Business Week*, February 8, 1993, pages 98–103.

The soul suffers: Thomas Moore, *Care of the Soul: A*

Guide for Cultivating Depth and Sacredness in Everyday Life (New York: HarperCollins, 1992), page 185.

Business process re-engineering: Michael Hammer, "Reengineering Work: Don't Automate, Obliterate," *Harvard Business Review*, vol. 68, no. 4, July/August 1990, pages 104–112. See also W. Edwards Deming, *Out of the Crisis* (Cambridge, Massachusetts: MIT Press, 1986); Joseph Juran, *Juran on Planning for Quality* (New York: Free Press, 1988).

Chapter 11

Law of requisite variety: Karl E. Weick, *The Social Psychology of Organizing* (Reading, Massachusetts: Addison-Wesley, 1979), page 189. See also Danny Miller, "The Architecture of Simplicity," *Academy of Management Review*, vol. 18, no. 1, January 1993, pages 116–138.

Incremental change: Tracy Goss, Richard Pascale and Anthony Athos, "The Reinvention Rollercoaster: Risking the Present for a Powerful Future," *Harvard Business Review*, vol. 71, no. 6, November/December 1993, page 98.

Dimensions of diversity: Marilyn Loden and Judy B. Rosener, *Workforce America!: Managing Employee*

Diversity As a Vital Resource (Homewood, Illinois: Business One Irwin, 1991), pages 18–19.

How to order the *Every Kind of Person* game;

Contact:
People Tech Consulting Inc.
154 University Avenue
Consulting – 3rd Floor,
Toronto, Ontario M5H 3Y9
(416) 596-8008

Chapter 12

Myth of work: Mihaly Csikszentmihalyi, *Flow: The Psychology of Optimal Experience* (New York: Harper and Row, 1990).